BEYOND THE BLOOD

MY BIGGEST FAMILY

DR. YADUVIR SINGH

Copyright © Dr. Yaduvir Singh
All Rights Reserved.

The book, "beyond THE BLOOD", is dedicated to the God, and to the entire humanity.

Contents

Foreword   *vii*

Preface   *ix*

Acknowledgements   *xiii*

Prologue   *xv*

1. Who We Are   1

2. From Where We Have Come   5

3. Why We Are Here   9

4. I Am Another You   13

5. The Real Me   17

6. The Nature   21

7. All Is An Illusion   24

8. All Physical Relations Are Fake   28

9. Our Relations And Relationships   32

10. I Am The Full Creation   35

11. Does God Exist   39

12. Did God Make Us   42

13. Who Made The God   46

14. We Are The Gods   50

15. Physical World And The Spirit World   54

16. Spirit Connections   59

17. Does Prayer Work   63

18. Beyond The Blood   67

19. My Biggest Family   71

20. The Biggest Religion   75

Contents

21. The Biggest Karma   78

22. Best Emotion   82

23. Best State Of The Mind   85

24. The Inner Transformation   89

25. The State Of Death   93

26. During The Death   97

27. After The Death   102

28. We Will Meet Again   108

29. Up In The Heavens   112

Foreword

The book, "beyond THE BLOOD" gives a clear and effective explanation of the real me, the God, spirits and the heavens. The book, "beyond THE BLOOD" is first book of its kind, which discusses all practical aspects related to the Physical World, death, the Spirit World, karma etc.. Spirits, death and karma always had been very interesting topics full of many secrets, and less understood by the majority of beings. Life and Karma is the essence of spirituality. Karma is the basis of whole creation. Thinking creates action(s). Thinking and action create Karma. The reader will get to know some amazing facts related to the relationships and the life after reading this book, "beyond THE BLOOD". The author has nicely sequenced and described the topics chapter wise. Body, mind and the spirit have been clearly explained. Afterlife has been described in a very clear and effective manner. People in general are ignorant of the design and secrets of the creation. Beyond the blood is one of the biggest secrets of the life, and must be lived with, for life's success. All enlightened beings live their lives same way. Yoga and meditation are the best ways to activate and train the subconscious mind. Meditation acts as a very precise better quality data filter, and thus, making a being, more mindful and happy than before. Death is actually not a loss. Beings always live in one's memory, subconscious and the unconscious mind. One can always reach to a dead loved one, through his or her subconscious mind. Inner talk establishes the communication with the dead being. Memories never die. Love never dies. Pain felt, is due to the love, but in the state of true love, i.e. the unconditional love, there should be no pain. Be thankful to the God, the nature, the existence for bringing that being in the life. Every being comes with his or her fixed journey of the life. Birth brings the death, and then, death brings the next birth, i.e. the rebirth, and thus, the drama of the life and the existence, goes on. Everything, every process is cyclical in the nature, and not linear.

This book, "beyond THE BLOOD" makes very lucid discussions about various scientific and spiritual aspects related to the life, relationships and the heavens. People working in the areas of psychology, cognition, neuroscience, religion and spiritualism will find this book as a ready reckoner and a guide, and an important handbook. Definitely this book is a very rich addition in the intellectual closet of the reader. In near future, some more good books on other life important and humanity related topics are expected from the author. The author, every other time, raises his own bar and the threshold, by creating another masterpiece, much to his name and credit. Spiritual beings do not run after success and glory, as it comes to them automatically due to their thoughts and actions. They are under constant divine guidance and blessings, and are being decreed by the God, to do the needed things in their given life.

Definitely, the readers will find it a very interesting book on this rare topic of beyond the blood, with many takeaways for their implementation in their daily lives.

- **Baba**

22 / 03 / 2022

Preface

This book, "beyond THE BLOOD" is a comprehensive discussion about the real me, relationships, the God, the Physical World, prayer, family, religion, karma, emotions, mind, death, afterlife and heavens. World of a being is the set of his or her life experiences. No two beings have similar experiences and learning, or similar life. Beings come into the existence to live by themselves, and to support others to live meaningfully. Life creates experiences. Life is an experience in itself. No bad experience is really bad. Discern and differentiate between the correct and the incorrect. A bad decision is just learning, which helps in the growth, evolution and advancement of the soul. In this creation, which is replete with duality, for every good thing, innumerable support logics can be mentioned, and similarly, for every bad thing, innumerable support logic can also be given, interestingly which may not be always incorrect. This journey of the life is not the end of the life. The life is a link in the eternal chain of our relationships with our love ones. Soul meets its friends and the relatives from the life they just lived after exiting its body. Souls, called "greeters", come and attend the dying being, and help him or her, in this transition, known as the death. Souls always exist in 'soul groups" or 'soul families", both in the Physical World and also, in the Spirit World. These souls often incarnate together. Souls share numerous lives, in the past, at the present, and also, in the future. There had been many reporting of seen and experienced spirits leaving together for the Spirit World after an accident. Spirit rises from its physical body. Spirit sees its dead physical body lying on the bed in the hospital

ICU, or lying in a pool of blood on road in an accident, or totally charred to death in a plane crash. It is the cover page photograph of this book. Also, two loving souls are also shown up in the heavens. There is a definite afterlife after the death on the other side. This creation has innumerable dimensions of its existence, with life everywhere, in all dimensions. We all are spiritual beings. We are here on the earth, temporarily for learning few allotted life lessons, which needs material form. Even, while living on the earth, one can meet his or her loved ones living in the Spirit World, in dreams. Dreams are gateways to spiritual realms.

Life is a game, understand it like a game only, and play it well. Mind is not a dustbin. Do not keep jealousy, hatred or anger into it. Mind is a treasure box. Keep sweet memories, happiness and unconditional love into it. Spending time on hobbies improves one's mental health, and also, the overall well-being. Practise various methods of spirituality and empower the self. Empowering the self is advancing the soul, which in turn, results in the start of one's journey on the path of reaching the God.

This book, "beyond THE BLOOD" is a great gift from the author to the entire humanity in today's times, when there is fierce professionalism, immense competition, tremendous fear, overwhelming stress, deepest levels of anxiety, weakest and most fragile bonds of relationships, heightened levels of distrust, hatred and lowest levels of mutual respect, high ego, no self-esteem and dignity, no integrity in actions, biases and prejudices, unethical practices and hypocrisy at their peak, and cynicism getting reflected all over in the human thought process.

This book, "beyond THE BLOOD" is a best pick of its times from bookstores, and a must read for all. I wish all the readers, a happy reading experience while going through every word, line, paragraph and chapter of the book, "beyond THE BLOOD". Reader will feel empowered while reading this book. Power is always of the soul. It is the power of the mind, which runs the whole show of life. Reader will not be able to stop, reading it again and repeating many chapters. Read and explain the book to the members of family, relatives and friends, and gift "beyond THE BLOOD" to them, and also, to the others.

- **Dr. Yaduvir Singh**
25 / 02 / 2022

Acknowledgements

The contents of this book, "beyond THE BLOOD" are the results of understanding and experiences of the author on this topic. However, one may always differ from that, what is written. Also, author tenders his sincere apologies in anticipation, if any content is contrary to their faith, belief, knowledge, information, experiences, and hurts their sentiment in any manner. The author will like to acknowledge, all visible and invisible forces, and powers of this existence for providing information, experiences, encouragement and support. The author will like to acknowledge all sources of information, which gradually developed author's understanding over many years, along with the experiences. The author also disclaims the responsibility for any loss or damage or harm, if any. Last but not the least, and also, much above everything and all, nothing is possible without the God's will. Author with full servility, respect, gratitude and surrender to the God, puts this book, "beyond THE BLOOD" on the feet of the God. All is of the God only.

Prologue

This book, "beyond THE BLOOD", is a gem in itself, a marvellous intellectual creation par excellence, and a must read book for all, and also, a worthy collection. It is a rare book on a very interesting topic i.e. life, relationships, soul's journey and heavens. This life, nature, universe and the entire creation are too intriguing and mysterious. This book, "beyond THE BLOOD" discusses real me, relationships, the God, the Physical World, prayer, family, religion, karma, emotions, mind, death, afterlife, the heavens, and many other important and relevant topics related to the life and the design of the existence. A reading of this book, "beyond THE BLOOD" will develop the reader's proper understanding about the real me, life and relationships, karma and the afterlife. The book, "beyond THE BLOOD" has given simple explanations of various aspects related to the mind, thinking, God and the journey of life. The reader will find the book too involving, informative, and also, recreational. Books are the best friends of human beings. Book makes a reader travel through all its contents, and experience the whole journey of reading by him or herself even without lifting the feet. Loosen up, and lose yourself in the book, "beyond THE BLOOD", find yourself there, and get benefitted in the life. Keep learning in the life.

CHAPTER ONE

Who We Are

Neither we are the bodies, nor the minds. We and our bodies are distinctly separate. Breath binds the real me to my body. Education is not just about the learning of the facts, but also, greatly about the right training of the mind to think correct and good. Life is a miracle. Every breath, which we take in and then push out, is the gift of the nature and the God to all of us. The problems of the life, and the sufferings in the life, are either the problems of the body, or the problems of the mind, or the both. Know the life. Thinking about the life, may not lead to knowing the life. Thinking and the thoughts create problems and sufferings. Thinking is the creation of the mind through thoughts. Thoughts are unreal, and keep on changing, as mind evolves. For a thing to be "real", it should be permanent. Knowing comes experientially. Once, we understand, "who we are", we will understand the life, and the life processes. God is an experience, and not a thought, in reality. "Thinking" must culminate into "experiencing" in order to become the reality. Thought is the seed, but its tree is the experience. Everything in the life, in essence is, what is experienced. Let it be, true knowledge, or the relationships, or even the existence. "Beyond the blood" is finding the true identity of the self; finding the real space and position of the self in this vast creation, and establishing the real relationships with every other thing here. "Beyond the blood" is the higher state of consciousness, when "I" dissolves, and "We" establishes. "Beyond the blood" is a profound constant feeling of integration in this creation. "Beyond the blood" is state of natural spontaneous universal empathy, i.e. empathy without discrimination. Everything is me only, in this creation. Sense of individuation is the source of all pains and miseries in the show and the game of the life. Enlightenment brings the real and true understanding about the life, and also about, "who we are". Know the nature of self-existence. "Who we are" is not an external seeking, but essentially an internal seeking. The knowing of "who we are" happens through inner journey. "Who we are" is an inner realisation and the experience. Meditation leads to this revelation, "who we are". At the spiritual level and the level of energy, all is me only. At the physical level and the level of matter or material, I am distinct from others. Physicality and matter or material is temporary, whereas, spirituality and the energy are permanent and constant. Choice is whether to go by temporary, or by the constant. "Who we are" is the question, which can never be answered at the physical level or at the level of matter or material, but can only be answered and understood at the spiritual level or at the level of the energy. The inner journey will also answer another related profound question, "Why we are here". We are the spirits, i.e. energies. We are vibrations. Whole creation is energy and vibration. God is also a vibration. Energies are never distinct, but one and the same. There is only one energy, with its innumerable manifestations, which are sense-perceived in this vast creation. The experiences of creation are the experiences of the life. I am everything, and everything is me. Essentially, I and others are no two different existences, but an incorrect experiencing by the body and the mind of the being. Mind creates thoughts and thinking. In essence, I am another you. I am everything, and everything is me only. Live in the state of all-inclusion, and not in the state of exclusion. Be open, and not close. Open is life. Close is death. Open and openness, is freedom, and also, the characteristic of every being's soul. Open is creation. Close is destruction. "Who we are" is the question, which must be answered in inclusiveness and openness, and not in exclusiveness and closed state. We are the nature. We are the elements of the God. We are the creation. We are the whole existence. We are the whole experience. Who we are, is an experience of the life. Life is forever. Life is infinite. We are ad infinitum. We are ever expanding with the expanding universe. We are the universe. We shall expand till infinity. The expansion of universe is the essentially the expansion of the self. When we expand, our experiences expand, and become real. The state of positivity, happiness, exhilaration is the expanded state of self, i.e. the state of expanded aura. Expansion is strength. Contraction is weakness. The question, "who we are" can only be answered in the expanded state of consciousness. Raise the level of consciousness, the question, "who we are", will get answered automatically by instinct or by gut. We are what we do. We are what we love. We are what we believe. We are what we give. We are how we interact. We are what we take. We are how we behave. We have no separate identity, but in essence a collective identity. Mistakenly and unfortunately, a majority of beings are trapped in the psychological game of their mind. Mind confuses and gets confused. "Who we are" is an experience, an experience above the body and the mind. It is not a question, but a very essential experience, of the life. Any experience will only come through experiencing. It will not come by discussing or listening, but only by doing, once read about it.

CHAPTER TWO

From Where We Have Come

From where, we have come? Why we are here? These are few other profound questions of the life, for which one must seek answers, and then only, life can be understood properly and celebrated. We all have come into the existence with the creation of this entire creation. We are individuated specks of cosmic energy. The cosmic energy is the God. We all had existed in this creation since infinite time in the past, and we all shall always exist here in this creation. This whole creation and existence is in the form of energy. This energy, from time to time, associates itself with the matter or the material, in order to assume physical form, and manifest itself. Body is physical. Soul is non-physical. Soul is energy. Body is matter or material. Over the time, our soul or the spirit, which is essentially the individuated speck of cosmic energy, tries to evolve, and for its evolution, it needs physical form for its manifestation. Karma is created, and also, dissolved easily in the physical form, than in the spirit form (energy form). Karma is essentially give and take of energies. Law of Karma is the Law of Equilibrium of these karmic energies. The purpose of this individuated energy (soul or spirit) is to get reunited with cosmic energy, in order to reach equilibrium. So, it (soul or spirit) travels from one birth to another, and so on in different times and spaces. As per the Law of Equilibrium, at equilibrium individual energy must reunite or get integrated with the cosmic energy. As long as this state of equilibrium is not reached, we are trapped, and this loop of birth-death-rebirth will go on. If all entities in this creation evolve to the highest state, this creation will cease to exist. Then, it will be the state of nothingness (Shiva). For birth, the soul or the spirit (i.e. the individuated cosmic energy; we) descend to the physical planes like earth. The purpose of each birth is soul's evolution and progress. Ultimately, the soul has to get reunited with the supreme energy, which will be state of salvation or Moksha or Nirvana. After a certain time of existence of us in the physical plane, the matter decays, and then the soul inside detaches itself with it, as the body can no longer contain it, and the purpose of this journey of life is over now. It is known as the death. Death is not an end, but start of a new journey. Death is not the end, but the beginning. Each journey of the soul is for its (soul's) further growth and development. After death, the spirit or the soul leaves for the higher or upper dimension or realm or plane. This higher dimension is called the Spirit World. There effects of time and space are negligible. Time moves very slowly in Spirit World, but the level of vibrations is very high. Physical plane like earth is a lower dimension or plane or realm. The soul descends on the earth to fast settle its karma, and to create this show of the life. Life on earth is a test life; therefore, there will always be more pains than the pleasures. Enlightened souls understand all this. They also understand the design of life. The physical plane like earth is a plane of lower vibrational level, but here, time moves very fast. There are innumerable such earths in this existence. There are many such universe, which is known as multiverse. After death, the soul or the spirit leaves for the Spirit World, where it is healed and prepared for next descend on the physical plane in the form its rebirth. There in the Spirit World, the soul or the spirit of being stays for some time, and then, at appropriate time and space coordinates with respect to the physical world, and as per its karmic accumulations, it again descends on the physical plane, which is called as its rebirth. Spirit or the soul, till it is not liberated, keeps shuttling between the Physical World (earth(s)) and the Spirit World. For the first time, we all have come from God, by the process of big bang, leading to our individuation, but then it comes every time from the Spirit World till its dissolution, and integration with the God. The state of dissolution is the state of complete bliss. There is no pain then, but only love and peace prevail. Being at his or her will can then reincarnate on physical plane, but he or she is not trapped in the loop of birth-death-rebirth. At complete dissolution, it ceases to have its separate existence. Being and the God become one then. We are here, in this and every life, for doing good karma, settling our karma, and finally, get liberated from this trap of birth-death-rebirth. We come here for our soul's evolution, i.e. growth and development. Everything here, is too ephemeral, constantly changing, therefore, nothing is for real. How a changing thing can be real. For something to be sense-perceived as real, it must become constant. But in this creating, change is the only constant. Uncertainty is certainty. The notion of life, as perceived by the normal beings is completely wrong. Everything, which happens, is pre-scripted. Life is a big drama. Nobody here is yours, and yet, all are yours. As a matter of fact everything is you only. It is your other form. Everything here, in this existence, as experienced, is you only. It is me only, in another form. Never do anything wrong and never hurt others consciously. Stop further creation and accumulation of negative karma. This creation and the whole existence, is based on strong causal (cause and effect) relationships. There is a very strong cause or a basis for everything or every effect, which is experienced in the show of the life. Nothing here is ad hoc, or random. Law of equilibrium of mass and energy (essentially, Law of Karma), is the bases of everything in this vast creation.

CHAPTER THREE

Why We Are Here

We are here to experience the life. Life has no distinct external purpose. Life is the purpose in itself, and the only reason for our existence here. We are here to live the life. We are here not by an accident, but by a certain cosmic design. Whole creation is the show of life. There is life all over. We come here only after the approval of the nature. If there is no life, there will be no creation either. God is the life. Life is the God. Life is a blessing. Life provides the ways for soul's unification with the God. When all the experiences of the life are over, we shall not be here, i.e. no further rebirths. Life is too short and very precious as well. Do not squander the life by squabbling. Remain happy and peaceful. Count the blessings. Be contented. Love family, friends and every other thing in this God's creation. Always smile. Make the most of every moment during the journey of the life. The ability to love and to care, are the gifts of God, to each one of us. Love and care are the words, which carry beauty in themselves, and immense potential to make the life rich and richer in true senses. Provide full and sincere care, from the heart. Care is not a play of mind, but an attribute of soul. Love is also a characteristic of the soul. Hatred is an evil, played by the mind. Carry the beings in your heart. Be real and sincere in behaviour. Never be dishonest. In life, nothing is for real. Birth and death are fictional. This whole creation works on perfection of certain geometry. This geometry has its various levels, which contains life in infinite forms. This geometry can also be defined in terms of time and space. If this geometry can be defined in terms of time and space, then everything in this creation can also be defined and understood in terms of times and spaces. Life started from water, and then it became terrestrial. Life is a certain process, and a continuous journey. We are here by a certain process of evolution. Do not worry about future. Live the present moment fully. Life is a drama, therefore, do the ways, as it works in the life, but remember every act must be approved by the soul. Realise the ecstasy and exuberance of the life. It is the very purpose of the life. Be happy. Being happy is an attitude. A right attitude towards the life brings happiness in the life. We create our own situations and circumstances of the life. Mind does it. Therefore, have a proper mind management during the journey of the life. We create joy, happiness and the bliss. We also create sorrows, pains, troubles and miseries. We are here to learn and grow and enrich the self, and also our world. We are here for stronger reasons and sincere purposes. Send and receive, love and care. We are here to help others to grow. We are here to create, and not to destroy. We are here to add something to the life, no matter small or big. We are here to nourish the true / real self. We are here, not to fear about the future, but to shape it well. We are here to settle our karma, and to create good karma. The exchange of energies between two beings must be positive. It simply creates a positive world around us. We are here to experience the nature and the God. We are here to simply celebrate the life. We are here to admire the creation and the creator. We are here to get inspiration from others, and to inspire the others. We are here for every good reason, and not even a simple bad reason. Think good, and also, act good. Learn from the mistakes. Forgive the self and the others for their mistakes. Do not linger negative matters. Forget the bad, and cherish the good. Our interaction with everything in our world should be good and adorable. The God must feel proud of us. Life is too good. Feel it, like it, and live it. Goodness to the life has to be given by you. We make our own life situations. There is nothing to lose in the life. As a matter of fact, with every loss, there is also some direct or indirect gain. In this God's creation, there is growth and progress only, always and all over. Change the perspective of the life, the life will change. Relations will improve with improved and right perspective of the life. Quality of the life also improves. In each one of us, lies some special gift, therefore use it, and contribute something good. We are here to smile, and make others smile. Be kind to others. Listen to all. Help, if possible. "Giving" comforts the soul. It heals the spirit. We are here for all good reasons, and to demonstrate the virtuosity. We are here to behave in all morally good ways. Organise the mind. Do inner journey, and get enlightened. Live in exhilaration. Practise silence. Silence will make the mind calm, and corrects the being's psychological patterns and settings. Silence is very powerful. Silence has the power to wash away all the anxieties and worries of the life. Practise yoga and meditation. Raise the energies within. Hone up the abilities of attention and concentration. It will help develop and improve further, the capacity of knowing and understanding. Without knowing the self, life and the creation cannot be known and understood. God cannot be experienced. We are here to know the self. Change the patterns of the life, if they are not in the right shape, and aimed in the right direction. We are here to consciously learn about the consciousness, which is the ultimate intelligence. Do not get trapped in the psychological game / play of the mind. Love yourself. We are here for no serious purpose, but for all sincere purposes. Respond to the life situations, and never react to these. We are here to demonstrate, the might like the Sun, and love, comfort and consolation like the Moon. We are here to give a touch to every being's life like the Wind. We are here to heal others like the Fire. We are here to comfort others like the Water. We are here to behave with dignity and magnanimity like the open Space. We are here to tolerate everything, and yet feed, bless, and beseech well-being of all others like the Earth. We are here to live with harmony and in completeness. We are here to interact, and to exhibit all the characteristics of five basic elements of the nature, which make us, viz. Earth, Water, Fire, Air, and the Space.

CHAPTER FOUR

I Am Another You

I am in everything, and everything is me only. I am another you. Most beautiful beings are the beings, which bring out the beauty in other beings. Also, you are another me. It is the highest level of empathy. It is the highest level of acceptance. It is the highest level of care, share and love. It is soul-to-soul connection, i.e. many bodies but one soul. "I am another you" is the most profound statement and a feeling. In essence, we all are same and one. This experience of "I am another you" makes the life and the world, very beautiful. Life then, finds its true meaning. Life becomes too beautiful. All enlightened beings had achieved this level of "I am another you". "I am another you" is the path from manliness to the godliness. Karmic accumulations then, are almost reduced to cipher. Karma is accumulated memory of this and all previous journeys of the life, which is being carried forward to each future journey of the life. Some karma are settled during the journey of life, but many new karma are being created. Thus, karmic accumulations for normal beings never become zero, and he or she remains trapped in the cycle of birth-death-rebirth. Karma is a big trap and reason for existence of this existence. Karmic accumulations can be reduced by conscious thoughts and actions. Improve and increase the levels of awareness and the consciousness. Do inner management. "I am another you" is a very high state of consciousness. "I am another you" is a universal feeling, when you are reflected in every entity of this creation, i.e. you become tree, bird, animal, river, mountain, stone, fish, water, fire, air, space, and everything. "I am another you" causes expansion of aura and consciousness. Being's vibrations become too intense. Aura turns white. Then communication starts with every other entity of the creation. "I am another you" thought's sharing and communication is quite necessary to harmonise the relations, and reach the equilibrium of life energies. "I am another you" is a transcendental experience, and the time and the space then, lose their significance and existence. Soulmates are such beings, which experience and live with the thought, "I am another you". Then, it makes the family big, bigger and the biggest. For enlightened beings, this world is their one family, i.e. the biggest family, and they are into everything, and everything is into them. Differences cease to exist then. It is the state of universal love, and the universality. Then, all the secret doors of the universe get opened, and the being becomes mystic, and eligible for extra-sensory perceptions. He or she then becomes a clairvoyant. He or she also has all paranormal experiences then. Such beings always live together, here in the Physical World, there in the Spirit World, and in all other planes or realms or dimensions of this vast creation. There is life, and only life in this whole creation. There is nothing like death, but just the transformations. Change is the very nature of this creation. Change is the life. Becoming constant is death. Such beings, which live the life with the thought "I am another you", shed their bodies together whenever they feel like, and then travel to the

Spirit World together, and live there together. Such beings walk the planet together. It is the illustration shown on the cover page of the book. After the plane crash, the spirit in the subtle body walks away from the site, and then spirits meet in the heavens. Their relations are simply "beyond the blood". They share and enjoy their biggest ever family. As a matter of fact, we all meet each other here in this Physical World, in the Spirit World in the afterlife, and other dimensions of existence in other times. Physical World, Spirit World and other worlds are spaces. Beings, which live with the thought, "I am another you", always feel one another, greet and meet each other, whether physically present or not. In essence, we all are vibrations. Our vibrational energies are always present in the creation. Nobody goes anywhere, or comes from anywhere. Only they go out, or come back into our sense-perception. Raise the level of sense-perception, the form will lose its significance, and then one can always contact the beings which are either in their spirit forms, or not available physically. Light, sound, smell etc. are the various forms of existence. "I am another you" is a state of sheer perfection, which is achieved though yogic practices and meditation. Then, one uses the visible and invisible powers of the universe, the way he or she wishes for. His or her acts look like a magic or a miracle to the normal beings. "I am another you" is the state of enlightenment. Telepathy, telekinesis, prophesying, time travel, astral travel, out of body experiences, near death experiences, materialisation, dematerialisation, simultaneous occurrence or existence at many places etc., become the normal abilities of such beings. For such beings, age is no bar. Soul or the spirit has infinite age. Every thought and every act, and then its result(s), is your responsibility. Shape up the life by conscious efforts. Give up all notions, judgements and conclusions. Live in expanded state of consciousness. Hold the sky. Embrace the space. Speak to the universe. Universe listens and responds. Every call is being answered. Help rushes, when solicited earnestly. Life is an experience, experienced by the being's soul or the spirit. Make smile a habit, and keep smiling always. Make your aura strong and the vibrations more and more positive. The negative and adverse circumstances and situations of life should not affect, deter, intimidate and discourage you; develop such a level of understanding. Life should greet the soul saying, "glad to meet you"; that should be the journey of the life, and the life experiences. Life is always sweet, sometimes not stirred up well, like a bitter coffee with sugar lying at the bottom of the coffee cup. Life never remains same. There are no set responses for life situations. For every being, life is unique, therefore somebody's prescription of the life will not work. Every being must explore and experience the life by him or her. "I am another you" is a very profound statement of the life, freeing the soul from the bondage and the shackles of the narrow mind sets and the negative games or plays of the mind, in order to soar high and high, and experience the freedom of thoughts and actions and universal brotherhood and all-acceptance. "Acceptance" is a responsibility, bestowed on each one of us by the God, to protect his creation with utmost love and care. Learn to share. "I am another you" is the thought of universal integration. The God also says to us, "I am another you"; therefore, let all of us prove worthy of it.

CHAPTER FIVE

The Real Me

A loyal being is always better than a royal being. Kindness always comes back. It is karma. We become, what we read, listen to, and watch and think. Therefore, be conscious, watchful, and apply wisdom, in exercising the choices and performing various actions. Nature is the God. Science is the truth. Humanity is the only religion. Work is the worship. One's actions must be directed at the well-being of the whole creation. Practise "pause" in life. Take pause before, assuming, judging and accusing others. Give time to time. Before reacting take pause in order to avoid regret and any guilt later. Life is too beautiful. Every day and every night is too beautiful. No event of the life is for real. All is just a dream and a drama. Enact in the show of the life, or take a ring side seat and witness it with aplomb, but always stay cheerful. The characteristic of soul is to stay peaceful and joyful. Be blissful. Success is connected with the actions. Successful beings keep moving. They do mistakes, but do not quit. We do not grow in the life, when the things are easy, but grow, only when we dare and face the challenges thrown by the time. Hard and harder is the challenge of the life, high and higher will be the growth in the life. Every day in the life needs not to be good, but there is certainly, something good in every day of the journey of the life. Life is all about a right attitude. Therefore, work on the attitude, if it is not right. A right attitude sees "good" in everything, every being and every situation. Most of the things in the journey of the life will not go the way we think or wish, therefore, accept these on the face of it, understand it, change it if you can, otherwise let it remain, and just move on. There will always much left in the life to be done, therefore, do not stick to a thing. A thing considered as bad for a being, is good for other being. Every confronted situation in the journey of life is all about how it is seen, and taken up; whether taken up as a problem for creating a pain, or taken up as an opportunity for self-growth and evolution. Happiness is inner joy. Happiness is all about striking the balance between wants and the possessions. It is not about how much we have, but all about how much we enjoy, which brings the happiness. Sufferings in the life are the way for realisation of the God. Learn to be happy with nothing, and you will be happy with everything in the life. Do prayers. Prayer is the spiritual oxygen, which we all need. Life needs not to be perfect in order to be wonderful. It is always wonderful, in all its forms and states always. Life is always perfect and wonderful, no matter what. Pain of yesterday is the strength of today. A being must be capable of translating other beings sorrow and silence into smiles. It is the best ever translation of the life. Everything is possible in this creation. What has not happened till today, may happen tomorrow. Every imagination and fiction is essentially a distant reality. A being can never imagine beyond the boundaries of possibilities. Manifest the wishes. Mind does the first creation for everything. Mind first creates an expression of that thing inside it, which has to be manifested. Mind creates our worlds. World is the set of experiences created during the journey of the life. Experiences depend upon, sense-perceptions, understanding and the attitude. We are the creation. We are the element of the creator. We make our own fate and destinies, and nobody else. We are, what our mind is. Therefore, mind management is quite important for a happy, successful and a meaningful life. Organise the mind. If the mind is organised, it shall also organise the remaining three subsystems i.e. physical body, emotions and the life energies. If mind, body, emotions and life energies are synchronised, then anything wished for can be manifested. "The real me" is, which can manifest anything by the organisation of the mind. Mind organisation is a tremendous empowerment of the being. Do not live in any confusion. Beings actions must be conscious, and not compulsive. Make the mind to work for yourself. Do not get worked on by the mind. Mind will make the life miserable, if not managed and organised. Have faith. Mind always try to weaken the faith. Mind creates doubts and fears. Mind develops anxieties. These are the pains of the life. Faith in me, makes, "the real me". Be simple minded. Never do overthinking. Unnecessary excess thinking is too self-destructive. Being becomes god, if the mind is managed well, and all the four energies i.e. mental energy, physical energy, emotional energy and the life energy are aligned. Make all efforts to achieve the set goals of life with full faith and efforts. Human spirit is all potent. Thought should be free of any negativity, and must be powerfully created. Such a created thought becomes reality. Our mental, physical, emotional and life energy states must be pleasant. Be the creator. Do not be destructive. Create a loving, joyful and a peaceful world through mind management. Great souls do have incurable ailments. They know the time, when they will leave their physical body. In the various pathological tests, no disease observations will be found, yet they get feeble and leave a day. It is the process of leaving the body. "The real me" inside knows everything, but the mind dupes and befools. No being is above the laws of nature. Law of abundance is also one of the many important laws of the universe. There is everything in abundance in this creation. Nothing is in scarce, therefore enjoy, and celebrate the life. "The real me" is immortal. Which is not me, has to be left a day. Do not create false associations in the life. "The real me" is the element of divine, and is pure and eternal. An understanding of "the real me" make the life a conscious choice, with its events consciously chosen and accepted, and not left just as accidental.

CHAPTER SIX

The Nature

Trees, birds, mountains, water, air, fire etc., all is me only, in other forms. God never says, "Understand me", but says, "Trust me". The creation is "my biggest family". The relations here are simply "beyond the blood". Soul or spirit needs "freedom". Understand the real meaning of this freedom, and do not get trapped in wrong understandings of freedom, as mind may play with it. Freedom in the life is the freedom for experiencing the life. It is the freedom for self-growth and soul's evolution. Experience the goodness of the freedom. Only good experiences add to the value of the life. No experience is bad for life. When we look for "good" in other beings, we are actually discovering the "best" in ourself. As a normal being, and leading a normal kind of life, one may not be able to see the pressures of other beings, and similarly, other beings may not be able to see the pains within us. For normal beings, it is the kind of their life, but it is not right. Whether it is about the work place or the family or the feelings of the friends, one must always try to understand each other a little more with every other time. One should try, seeing and understanding, the situation(s) from other being's point of view. Try putting yourself in other's shoes. One must learn to think, and act, differently. One should be more and more open to other being's perspectives and opinions. Always, a little kindness and patience go a very long way in the journey of the life in the benefit of the being. Beings, which we meet in the journey of life, might be fighting their own battles of their journey of life. Some beings, even we will never hear about. We wish that other beings should be more understanding, and also, compassionate and helpful to us. So, we do all bad things to the other beings. For a happy, successful and meaningful journey of the life, learn practising "pause". Take a pause, before assuming others. Take a pause, before accusing others. Take a pause, whenever we are about to react harshly. By taking pause, one avoids saying things, which he or she will otherwise regret later. Always be kind to each other, others and every other entity in this magical and marvellous creation. Look deep into the nature, in order to better understand the self and the whole existence. Nature brings peace to the mind. Nature smiles in many ways. Light and colours are the smiles of the nature. Flowers are the laugh of the nature. Light and zephyr are the healing touch of the nature. Rain is the embrace by the nature. Rushing water is the music composed by the nature. Experience the nature in all its forms and ways. Everything which we see in the nature is our family, one family, "my biggest family". Life is just awesome and wonderful. Live with the nature, the nature's ways. Like and love the nature. Difficulties in the life are like a baggage, heavy for those who see it, and light for those who handle it. Learn all this from nature. Nature is the art of the God. Nature is the combination and the repetition of all of its laws. Real relationships are never carnal, but exist at the level of the souls, i.e. simply, "beyond the blood". Real relationships are never based on matter, but based on energies. One's relationships with the nature are beyond the blood. He, who created the nature, has also created all of us. We and the nature are two forms of the same creation, created by the creator. Thoughts and the actions should be all-inclusive and never ever exclusive. Inclusivity brings peace and strength to the mind and to the soul, whereas exclusivity disturbs the peace of the mind and simply saps the being. This creation works on universal consciousness, where every being contributes to the making of this consciousness. Collection of individual consciousness is universal consciousness. What one thinks and acts, reaches across the whole universe, and thus, perceived by every entity. Lasting feeling of happiness, in essence, is always collective. Happiness of individual only, is always fleeting. God is the friend of the silence, and can only be experienced in the silence. Practise the inner-silence. Do mind management. Do meditation. Do yoga. Do prayers. Nature is the only place to get healed up, and also, getting recharged. Whole knowledge lies within the nature. All magic lies within the nature. Nature does miracles. Human knowledge is simply the collection of experiences and the observations of the events, which keep happening in the nature. Nature is too affectionate and loves everything. Nature teaches. Nature punishes. Soothing effect of nature is unparalleled. Nature puts all the senses of beings back in the order. Nature teaches patience. Nature is never mute, but always, keeps on talking, communicating and teaching. Nature is simple, and teaches simplicity, i.e. simplicity of understanding in the life, in the relationships, and in thoughts and actions. Experience, consider and learn fully, the nature's gestalt.

CHAPTER SEVEN

All Is An Illusion

Life is a big illusion. Life is a trap. Death is an illusion. Birth is an illusion. Nothing is for real here. Only if, a being knows the life, then only, he or she knows the birth and the death. If one knows the birth and the death, then only he or she also knows the life. No experience here is for real, and permanent. It is a continuously changing cosmos. Life here, changes every moment, and so are the situations and circumstances associated with the life. What is here today, will not be here tomorrow. What is not here today, will be here tomorrow. You, me and everything, which we sense-perceive do not remain same the very next moment. Remain very happy in the life, and let others become happy too, when they meet and greet you. Life is, what happens, when you are planning. Do not make fun of anyone in the life, because one day you might also be in the same life situation. Life does not come with a manual. Life only comes with a mother. Mother is the God sent angel on the earth before the being. Live the life. Live all the relations, and enjoy the sweetness of various relationships. Have "giving" attitude. Only rich and wealthy can give. Live with an open mind, with the notion of "Beyond the blood", and considering this vast creation as, "my biggest family". We all are spirits. We all are energies. We do not have any thing fixed in the life. Life is a kaleidoscope. In physical form, we are manifestations of a short duration association of matter and energy. Life is infinite. Life is a continuous journey. Matter is composed of five elements, known as Panchamahabhutas. Matter consists of five basic elements, viz. earth (prithvi), water (jala), fire (tejas), air (vayu), and the space (akasha). Among all these, subtlest is the space, and grossest is the earth, with every perceptive sense. All perceived problems of the life are an illusion. Everything is a lie in the life. Life is best for those beings that enjoy it, difficult for those beings that try analysing it, and worst for those beings that criticise it. Beings attitude creates the paths or the ways of his or her journey of the life. Thoughts and emotions, which are the projections of life, chiefly compose the life. Emotions are created out of thoughts. Thinking creates feeling(s). An emotion is intense than a thought. Emotions are slow but long prevailing thoughts. "Beyond the blood" is a feeling. "My biggest family" is also a feeling. Both, "Beyond the blood" and "My biggest family" create sweet emotions. Sweet emotions make the life sweet. Only, a sweet life is a happy life with meaning and worth. Material life has no value. Time is an illusion. Past, present and future exist together. Perceived reality is an illusion, which is agreed upon by the majority. "Beyond the blood" and "My biggest family" create the biggest sphere of attachments, which is all-inclusive. "Beyond the blood" and "My biggest family" are unifying and holistic in essence. Body and mind create attachments. Mind is an accumulation, i.e. an accumulation of tendencies of the past and the present. Right attachments bring happiness in the life, and the wrong attachments bring miseries and sufferings in the life. Detach yourself from the thing, which troubles you. Troubled mind is the curse of life. Though mind is a closed possibility, however, it can be made open, by learning, unlearning and re-learning. Learning must be right in order to have a right mind. Learning creates impressions of the mind. Mind is subtle impression. These impressions only create the mind. Always establish the right basis before acting. We all are alive and dead simultaneously in the life in infinite parallel universes, which create this life and the existence. Being's consciousness belongs to the universes, and not to him or her. We all are immortal beings, and essentially exist outside the time and the space. Explore the life, beyond the survival, as mere survival is not enough. Do not limit life's possibilities. Access all the dimensions of the life. There are lower and higher dimensions of existence. In physical body, a being lives in his or her three-dimensional frame of existence, which is a lower dimension. This three-dimensional frame of existence is not the only frame of existence, but there are other frames of existence too. Therefore, experiences of any one frame of existence are incomplete, and create only an infinitesimal fraction of magnitude of the all possible experiences. Considering gathered experiences of this life, as the experiences of the life, is grossly mistaken, fallacious and illusory. Live the life in magnanimity. Everyone is yours, and everything here is also yours. In turn, you also belong to everybody. Set aside and abandon parochial thinking and life approaches. Scale-up the level of experiencing, and experience the life to its maximum possible. Be kind, generous, loving, helping, forgiving, forgetful, creative, docile etc. in order to gain the richer experiences of the life. Nothing is permanent and real here in the show and the game of the life, as all is an illusion. The existence of the existence is the only reality. This existence is the God. We are the elements of this existence, which keep changing and evolving continuously, as per the laws of the existence. The cosmic design is definite at a moment, but keeps changing. Since moment cannot be perceived and defined, therefore, cosmic design is almost beyond the comprehension, and so is the life.

CHAPTER EIGHT

All Physical Relations Are Fake

All relations at the physical level are simply fake and unreal. Only, spiritual relations are true and real. True and real relations are created at the levels of souls and spirits. Such beings, with their relationships at the levels of souls or spirits always stay and live together in all the dimensions of existence i.e. times and spaces, including the earth and also the heavens. Death is the process of transformation. Real love is spiritual, as opposed to the physical. At the time of death, such being walks away, out of this dimension, i.e. physical world, earth, and re-joins the soulmate in the heavens. It is the cover story of this book. Their relationships are heavenly, and simply, "beyond the blood". There is a definite journey of the souls. This whole creation is the biggest family for those beings, which live their relationships at soul's level, i.e. beyond the blood. In essence, a relationship is a necessary understanding. Understandings can never be absolute, but are always variable in the nature, and so are the relationships i.e. varying in nature, as relationship emerges out of understanding. Relationship has to be conducted every time, and also, needs conscious care and attention. Though, life is an illusion in itself, but still, try living the life, and also, living the relations and the relationships in the life, in disillusioned states. Do not live in the illusory state of believing, in the case of relationships. Beliefs in the case of beings are bound to be broken at some point of time in the life. Therefore, be adaptive, and adjust with the relations. Hope gives victory over despair. Do not fear anything in the life. The only thing, one should always fear of in the life is fear itself. Dare to initiate. Dare to propose, and dare to begin good things, especially in the relationships. Everything is a big lie at the physical level; therefore, try disposing the things from the deeper levels of the psyche. Involvement in the things, and other physical transactions, must be sincere, deep and deeper. Never try extracting anything from the relationships. Real relationships are based on attributes of, being together, caring and sharing. Let the life, blossom to its completeness for one and all in the creation. Relationship is an element of the life, and not the complete life. Relationships in the life are designed and created, by the divine to teach the things that are not learnt so far in the life. Learning only happens in hardships. Relationships are based on the kind of exchange of energies, i.e. karmic balances on the side of each other. Relationships must bring positive transformations. Life is a test. Relationships are the questions of this test, and the test has to be compulsorily taken by every being in the journey of life at some stage. Being's connect with the God is also the relationship between him or her, and the God. Relationships must be consciously understood. Relationships are necessary to live the life. Our relationship with the nature should also be good. Relationships are the opportunities of the life. Relationships bring forth the realities of the life. One must learn and improve him or herself, from his or her relationships, which get created in the journey of life. Type of present relationship is created out of past memories, and the present relationships create memories for future. There are several types of memories. Physical body has its own memory. Mind has memory. Relationships involve emotions like joy or sadness, or love or hate, and these emotions are powerful, and greatly affect the quality of life. Relationships should not be based on opinion(s). Relationships should have nurturing outcomes. Relationships should not bring in dependability, yet there should be full connectedness. Maintenance of relationships needs lots of conscious efforts. Let the mistakes do not soil and spoil the relationships. Relationships exist in the mind. Relationship management is mind management. Give up all foregone conclusions and foredrawn judgements. Eliminate biases and prejudices. Learn to live in the present state. Improve it later, if needed. Learn to handle the emotions. Do Yoga to bring the balance in the life. Our life is our making. We write our own destinies. One's life can be changed by his or her conscious efforts, i.e. conscious thoughts and actions. One's Karma is one's creation. Karma is, action done. Be patient, practise faith and belief. Give time to the time. Develop proper understanding. Love is not attachment. Love can be healthy or unhealthy. Attachment makes the beings impatient, and gives lots of pains. Attachment makes one's mind to depend on other's mind. Dependency of any kind in the life is not good. Dependency is a weakness. Do not become victim of your own expectations. Practise detachment. Detachment is unconditional love, and all-acceptance. Detachment is normal. Attachment is abnormal. Attachment and detachment both, occur in the mind. Always radiate the energy of pure unconditional love, no matter what.

Overcome fear, uncertainty and doubts. Infuse and maintain enthusiasm in life. It all needs a purposeful thinking, and a right mindset. Never let the despair to dominate in the life, celebrate the abundance of love, happiness, joy and the good health. There is nothing tough and discouraging in the life. Life simply means experiencing. Do not give importance to the tough life situations and life circumstances. Do not discuss these even. Never think about these. Always in the life and the nature and the surroundings, there is lots of good happening all the time everywhere. Always, be grateful. Be grateful to the God for all that, which you have been bestowed upon in the life i.e. good health, good family, good friends, good relations, good job, decent house and needed wealth etc.. Blessed is the being, which understands that prayer is not asking for more and more in the life, but it is simply an act of thanksgiving to the God for all that, which the God has already given to him or her in his or her life. Everything wished for, will definitely not come in the life. No being has got it. But, believe that the God has a secret very good plan for every being. Have faith in the self and the God. Already the God has given many things. Leave the gains to the God, make sincere efforts. Live the relations at the level of the souls, as only these relationships are for real, and all physical relations are simply fake. Physical relations are not going to exist. Physical relations exist as long as the physical body exists, but relationships created at the levels of soul and spirit persist, even when this physical body is gone, i.e. we are gone.

CHAPTER NINE

Our Relations And Relationships

Real and true relations and relationships cannot be logically examined and evaluated. Such relations and relationships, which can be examined and evaluated, are unsustainable. Our relations and relationships are between, two minds, two emotions, and the two bodies, which can never match, and fit perfectly. Our relationship with all elements of nature and creation must be at the highest levels of truth and goodness. Magic of being together is inexpressible, and simply cannot be contained in the logic. Nice beings live in memory. Better beings live in dreams. Sincere beings live in the hearts. This is a living cosmos. And, the life is a cosmic happening. Relations and relationships bind the cosmos. Karma creates relationships, and relationships create Karma. Karma has no set menu. Creation serves a being, what he or she best deserves. Change is the life. Becoming constant or getting stagnated is death. Make relations and relationships true and pure with the help of Ho'oponopono Manifestation Technique. It is a very powerful technique based on Law of Attraction. Ho'oponopono Manifestation Technique involves four affirmations, viz. "I am sorry", "Please forgive me", "I love you" and "I thank you". Ho'oponopono Manifestation Technique does deep healing by re-wiring the mind. It is the technique for forgiveness, reconciliation and the self-transformation. One's relations and relationships need his or her continuous attention. Relations and the relationships need continuous reassurances and renewed sincere commitments and involvements without trifles and frivolities. Good relations and relationships are blessings in the life, and are based on past and present Karma. Good and sincere relations and relationships are created through divine intervention. We act as per our memories, tendencies and the impressions. Mind is the heap of impressions. Take good sleep. Sleep is a natural meditation. Meditation is a conscious sleep. All relations and relationships are created in the heavens. All relation and relationships are created in the Spirit World. Here, in the Physical World, we only live these relations and relationships, and gather experiences from these. Every entity in this vast creation is in relation and relationships to other entities. One affects all. Relations and relationships are exchange of energies among the souls. Energy and vibrations travel the whole cosmos. These energies and vibrations do not die, but always exist. The cosmos is vibration. God is also a vibration. Inclusiveness is the key to a happy and meaningful life. Manage the relations and relationships of the life. Know the secrets of happy relations and the relationships. One's thoughts, feelings, spoken words and behaviour create his or her relation(s) and relationship(s). Focus on yourself, and not on others. Love yourself. Do not abuse self-mind. Release the past. Discuss the solutions, and not the problems. Never create negative thoughts. Difference of opinion should be kept up to discussions only, and not brought into the behaviour.

Love others unconditionally. Work on emotional independence. Think right no matter what. Eliminate all fears of the life, i.e. fear of any kind. Fear is death. In essence, fear of death is also no fear, as death never occurs. Fear is a play of mind. Overcome it. Release regret and guilt. Learn to live without the loved ones. Life is a show, a drama; in every journey of life, a new time period, a new space, a new script, a new role, a new stage and a new set of the co-actors. Attachment is not love. Love and respect yourself. Do not overthink. Keep control on the self. Without communication, there is no relationship, therefore, keep healthy communication in order to maintain a healthy relationship. Without respect, there is no love. Relations and relationships require commitment, patience, persistence, love and loyalty. Wrong relationships teach recognising the right relationships, when they arrive. There are no assumptions in real and true relations and relationships. Relationships go through struggle(s), but, only strong relationships get through it and ultimately survive. Being does not need someone to complete him or her, but someone who accepts him or her completely. It is real and true relationship. Trust is the glue of all relations and relationships. Family is not about the blood, but something simply "beyond the blood", and about, who is willing to support you and hold you, when you need it most. Good relationship is based on accepting the past, supporting the present, and encouraging the future. Feel the sweetness of relations and relationships with right understanding. Remember that other's efforts are reflections of their interests in you. Real and true relations and relationships appreciate the similarities, and also, respect the differences. Real and true relations and relationships are always motivational and inspirational.

CHAPTER TEN

I Am The Full Creation

See one in all, and all in one, i.e. my biggest family. Nature is the art of the God. Life is creation. Life is created, and not found. Journey of the life is the journey, directed towards its creator. Attract in the life, which you want in the life. God always prepares us for more and more, every time. Trust the prayers. Choose the emotions consciously. Clear all the past Karma. Beauty lies in the diversity. This creation is too diverse. Always, listen to the soul, as it is older than the heart, and also, wiser than the mind. Being's relations and relationships are too diverse. Do not expect others to be the same, think same, speak same, and also, act and behave same. Diversity makes the life, and also, the whole creation, very beautiful. Refine the communication. Boost brain power. Enhance the life. Live to the fullest. I am the full creation. This creation is, what I am. My world is set of my own experiences. One's creation is his or her creation. The creation finds its place and meaning, as long as, I shall exist. We are not just limited to this physical body, or family, or friends and relations, or colleagues and the neighbourhood, but we all extend from minus infinity to plus infinity in our existence. One's experiences of the life and creation are the experience of being's within. Live in magnanimity, i.e. in the expended state of consciousness.

Expansion is life, contraction is death. In every struggle, there are hidden blessings. Trust that being in the life, which finds, sorrow behind smile, reason behind silence and love behind the anger. Creation and the creator, i.e. the God, are same. The creator resides inside every element of its creation. God resides within all of us. Therefore, I am the full creation. Mind tries to create a sense of separation and detachment of being from the creator. Manage the mind in the positive direction. Without blessings of the creator, life is simply not possible. Life cannot exist. This life is God's will and the gift. Do not limit yourself to your physical possessions and physical abilities. Rise above the physical. Physical possessions have no worth and value over the spiritual possessions. Be spiritually accomplished. Being the superior species, we have much greater responsibility to help all others, other species, and protect this creation through pious thoughts and actions. Act consciously. Praise the God for his every act, decision and effects thereof on the life. Do not worry. Do not avoid the life. Learn to enjoy the suspense. Make life experiences profound and intense in order to live the life meaningfully. Manage the life energies in order to affect the life and the destiny. Have control over thoughts, emotions, body and the energies in order to have control over the life and the destiny. Physical processes are cyclical in nature, which means bond, i.e. the compulsive state. Do not live in the bondage, but live free. Do not make judgements or conclusions. Life neither can be judged nor concluded. Judgement and conclusion, is not knowledge. Knowledge is remaining open to the newer dimensions and possibilities, adventures, and finally new experiencing. God is also an experience of the life. In the life, everything is just an experience. All relations and relationships are experiences.

Thoughts and actions are experiences, and also, further create newer experiences. Experience living "beyond the blood". Experience the full creation as "my biggest family". It will make the life, full and perfect, happening and vibrant. Do not be limited, but become unlimited, i.e. the limitless. Learn to make right conclusions and the right decisions. Make yourself unshakeable. Be emotionally, mentally and physically stable. Reactions are the cause of sufferings, therefore, never react but always respond. Free yourself of all fears and insecurities of the life. Fear is death. Use techniques of manifestations for changing and shaping the life. Stay motivated and inspired all the time during the journey of the life. Set your own sky, and take the flight accordingly. Do not limit your sky. Sky is the limit of possibility. Only, we have the answer to our every problem, and nobody else. Accept the situation(s) in order to overcome the sufferings of the life. Acceptance is a too powerful thought, emotion and the action. Say no to overthinking. Change negative thoughts and live a tension-free and a worry-free life. Life is always perfect in its all forms. Universe will not work and behave the way, the mind works and behaves. Suffering is due to the conflict between the mind and the acts of the universe. Make the mind to accept the realities of the life. Many things in the life, in the case of normal beings only exist in their minds, and not in the reality, which leads to delusions and doubts. Thing happening in the mind is called fantasy. Life as designed by the God is like the flow of a river. Accept the direction of the flow of the river of the life, in order to avoid the sufferings of the life. Never blame the God. Take actions, where it is appropriate to take the actions. God says to act, and do the best possible in every life's situation and the circumstance. Let us do our job, and the God will do his job, and then, fully accept the consequences, in order to live the life happily and in the state of contentment. Contentment is the key to happiness. It brings peace of mind, and finally the peace in the life. Do not become a permanent victim of life's circumstances. Rise, and fight for the right. Changes are brought or created in the life. Destiny is created. Life can be partly controlled, and partly uncontrolled. The uncontrolled portion of the life is controlled by the universe. In essence, there is nothing uncontrolled in the life. Life cannot go the uncontrolled way. If we do not control our part, life will automatically take charge of it, and will control it. Normal beings do not live beyond the blood. Normal beings do not create their bigger and bigger, i.e. the biggest family. Their minds restrain them from thinking and doing so. Mind tends to make the life miserable. All is just oneness. I am the creation. Creation is me only. I and the creation are not distinct and separate. Live in the state of integration and fullness, with the nature, the creation, the universe, and the cosmos. Fullness brings in completeness. Choose the positive, and not the negative. Rise above the individuality. Individuality is the reason of pain(s) in the life. Learn to surrender. Eliminate the ego, for all its negative effects and bearings on the life. Life is a game. Give up unnecessary desires, and the self-importance. Control the habits, especially those, which are unwanted. Happiness lies within all of us. Divinity lies within us. I am the God. I am the full creation.

CHAPTER ELEVEN

Does God Exist

It is one of the inevitable questions of life – Does God exist? Yes, God exists, but not in the form, as usually portrayed by the beings. God is not a belief, but an existing reality. Supreme energy of this cosmos is the God. The energy of the universes is the God. It is the energy, which controls everything in this creation. God is the vibration. We are also vibrations. Every single entity in this creation is a vibration essentially. The physical form of things is due to the energy association with the matter. The energy of the universe remains in the form of vibrations only. God is beyond essence and existence. Beings have created the concept the God. Thought has created the God. Thought worships the image of the God, which the thought itself has created. The notion of the God, as created by the beings, has been created out of fear, and for their security, and for their patronage. God is an abstraction. God is an eternity beyond the limits of time and space. God cannot be imagined by the beings. A disbeliever of the existing concept of the God is the right and true believer of the God, as the God cannot be simply sense-perceived by the five senses, but is only experienced in a certain state of the mind, body and the spirit. God is not some kind of insurance, as usually treated by the beings. God gives every single thing in the life, which is needed and best deserved by the beings, even without asking him for it, i.e. without any prayer. God treats all equally, whether some being believes in him, or simply does not believe in him. God is the nature. God is the whole existence. Nature and existence, has its own laws. Laws of the nature and the existence are based on love, care, protection and correction, and no retaliation. The God made multiverse, i.e. parallel universes. There are 84 universes. Every morning in the life, beings are reborn i.e. it is a rebirth. Forget all bad moments of the life of past, forgive all those who did something bad to you, and make today, the most beautiful day of the life. Not every being makes it to your future. Some beings are just passing through, to teach you the lessons of life. Love yourself and release the hurt. Take charge of your time, space and the life. Never explain yourself to anyone, as the beings, which like you do not need your explanation, and, the being, who dislikes you, will not believe, even after listening to you. Those beings who judge you, will never understand you, and those beings, who understand you will never judge you. Beautiful tomorrow never comes, as when it comes, it has already become today. Therefore, in the search of beautiful tomorrow, do not trifle away your wonderful today. Do not plan too many things, as the God, who has given the life, has his own best plan for you. Remember that, most the beautiful moments of the life were actually unplanned, and same is going to happen in the future also. Happiness is enjoying the little things of the life. Timing is the key. The God has given each embryo, its own unique genetic identity, and perfect and out-and-out form and the format. The God is the chief architect, i.e. the supreme energy, which created this vast cosmos, and its things. The God manifests itself in the form of this perceivable existence, and the non-perceivable existence. The God is the cause of everything, and beings and every other thing are simply the effects.

CHAPTER TWELVE

Did God Make Us

Does God exist? Why are we here? What is the purpose of life? Who created the God? Can God be experienced? What is God? Should we pray the God? Did God make us? These are few of many questions, which haunt beings from time immemorial. Self-realisation and enlightenment give answers to all these questions of life. Pay attention to the question, "Did God make us?", and the universe will open its doors, and the answer will be found. Answers for all questions are present in the universe. Universe contains complete knowledge. For sure, we did not make ourselves, then who. All questions, and also, their answers, are available here in the universe. Self-realisation is, knowing the self by paying enough and adequate attention to this dimension of the life. The source of creation throbs within all of us. God made us, and also, other life forms, to enjoy this creation, complete this creation, and in all this process, also to grow and to evolve. As every play or act needs audience, so, we were needed here, for this nature, and for this creation. Human form of the life emerged as an advancement of other life forms, which is equipped with all needed faculties, which could bring it near to the God, i.e. make beings "god-realised". Spiritual growth is the purpose of the life, for which the God made us. First step towards any change is awareness, and the second step is acceptance, so get aware and then accept the facts of the life. Best preparation for tomorrow is, doing the best possible today. Always fill yourself with the positive thoughts. Life and love are the wonderful gifts given to all of us by the God. Best philosophy of the life is to keep the mind happy and peaceful. Success may not bring happiness. A happy and peaceful mind always leads to success first, and the happiness next. Use full wisdom. Wake up, shake up, break up, and then, make up yourself. You have come a long way, from who you were, to who you are now. Some things have been chipped away, and many things have been polished. All along the journey of life, at every step and every turn, a new facet of you has revealed itself, each, as brilliant as the last, each, a sparkling tribute to yourself and the God. Appreciate yourself. Be proud of yourself. Thanks the universe for everything, which you have got till date. More will come. Keep going. Love and blessings of loved ones are always there without saying. Celebrate the life. Be happy, cheerful and peaceful always. God is within us. Parents and all loved ones are within us, and not outside. We cannot solve a problem by using the same thinking, which had created the problem. Therefore create a right thinking with mind management, Yoga and meditation. Like and love all. My commitment is only my commitment. If somebody helps, well, otherwise, very well. Do not judge others. No negative thoughts of any kind. Be wise, act wise. My world is purely my world, and my loved one's world. All are also welcome in my world. Nobody can disturb me. Only, I am, the controller, maker and shaper, of my life. Time does not wait for anybody. Time does not stop for anybody. Excuses will not slow down the time. Indecisions will not delay the time. Complaining will not stall the time. Regrets will not turn back the time. Never waste time in anger, regrets, worries and hate. Time will not turn back, and cry along with you. It is time, let go off the past, and stop worrying about the future. The only time is the time now. Make sure to spend the time with the right purpose, with right deeds, with right emotions, with right thoughts, and with the right beings. Time flies. One can always spread his or her wings and soar with the time, and navigate the life, in the best possible ways. One never passes the same way again in the journey of the life. Count the time. Do what the time does, i.e. keep moving. Problems in the life create the music of the life. Life is never easy, but we have to make it easy, sometimes by ignoring the things, and, sometimes by accepting the things. Love all and like all. Create good and reliable friends in the journey of life. One honest voice of a friend is louder than a million fake ones. The world suffers a lot, not because of the violence of bad beings, but because of the silence of the good beings. A 'No' uttered from the deepest conviction is far better than a 'Yes', merely uttered to please or to avoid a trouble. The supreme energy of this creation is the God. The God created everything. As the capstone of his works, the God also created beings in his image. The God shares his overflowing love, grace and goodness with everything in this vast creation. God is perfect. God has no lack. God has an incredibly valuable task for each one of us. God creates situations of the life, unique for each being, in order to carry out his will on the earth. Being's job is to prove how good and acceptable and perfect the God's will is, so that in future, it is incontestable. God has carefully, fearfully, wonderfully and individually made each one of us. As the God thought of us, and also, created all of us intentionally, therefore, we need to understand the God's purpose for the lives, which the

God has given to us.

CHAPTER THIRTEEN

Who Made The God

Human beings coined the word "God". God is in their sense-perception. God is in their faiths and beliefs and understanding. For some, God exists, and for many others, God simply does not exist. Human beings created the image of the God, and the understanding about the God. God made the man in his own image, and in return, man made the God in his own image. But, God made the man, and itself. Nature creates the nature. Beings create beings. Similarly, God created the God. As a matter of fact, it is not a new creation today, but simply a re-cycling or a transformation or metamorphosis of that, which had existed before today. God has no beginning and no end. When there is no beginning, there is no point of creating or making. When there is no end, there is no point of destroying. God for him is beyond any construction and any destruction. Something which can be made can also be destroyed. Since, the God, as understood, cannot not be destroyed, therefore cannot be made also. Therefore, the question, "Who made the God" is irrational with no purpose, meaning and the worth. As a matter of fact, beings create the life, as life is an outcome of the karma, i.e. being's karma. Truth is very often more stranger than the fiction. God made the time, the space, matter and the energy. All human experiences are based on defining, depicting and attracting. Infinite is hidden in the void. This infinitely vast existence is a void. Infinity and zero are complementary to one another, and just cannot be separated; else they will cease to exist. Infinity and zero are the same. Point of zero is also the point of infinity. God is infinite. God is void. God is the cause of all causes. Every day dawns with new life and new hopes in this world drama. Doing good to the others is always a joyful act, which improves one's own health and increases his or her happiness. Smile more and more. Do what excites you. Create beautiful memories. Appreciate all little things of the journey of life. Life is incessant, a continuous journey. Life is an opportunity to become good, do good and get the good. Life is as simple as we allow it to be. Beings strive to create the spaces for their existence, and expect appreciation from the others, and try to dominate the others. Beings possess ambitions in the life. Family, relatives, friends and society create the space for the being, and also appreciate him or her, but dominance on others and achieving the ambitions is purely done by the being. The moment one accepts the responsibility for everything happening in the life, he or she gains the power to change anything of his or her life. For peace of mind, stop fighting with the thoughts. Have good friends in the journey of life. Wealth is not the permanent friend of life, but friends are the permanent wealth. If something can be dreamt, it can also be done or achieved, as all limits are within the self. Limitations are constraints and fears created by the mind, which can be very easily overcome with the help of certain practises. Do not cry, but try. Crying collapses confidence, whereas trying builds the confidence, therefore keep trying, and keep making the efforts. Understand how time really works. Be the owner of your time. Learn how to get real and true empowerment in the life. Control the life energies. There are various simple techniques and methods about it. Use the power of the angel number 1176. Angel number 1176 is for focus and attention, and signifies that beings have certain bestowed and endowed gifts by births present in their lives, and they must use them in order to become successful. Law of Attraction, Use of Affirmations, Water Technique, Tratak, Kundalini, Meditation etc., are such life transforming and empowering techniques and methods. In life, everything is just an experience. Explore and experience. God is also an experience. Our family, relations, society, physical objects etc., are either experiences in themselves, or simply the tools for creating the experiences. Life is too short. It is not what we have in life, but who all we have in the life. Take time to celebrate the life, and appreciate the amazing beings who are present in the life. Every created thing needs to have a creator. As darkness is the absence of light, similarly problems in the life are simply the absence of ideas of finding their solutions. No problem, as a matter of fact, is a problem in the life. Changes and challenges come in the game or the show of the life, not to discourage the being, but to give him or her more strength, and to make him or her more profound and experienced and wiser than the before, and eventually, making his or her life, quite happening and interesting. Do not follow the majority every time, but always follow the right ways in the journey of the life. Thoughts and actions must be consciously created and done. God is love. God did not create the universe; rather he himself becomes the universe. Creation, sustentation and transformation of the cosmos are eternally ongoing processes. There was no beginning. Also, there will be no end. Here, in this vast creation, everything is just the eternal dance in the present. All is happening here, and now. God never ever had a creator. God was not created by something. God is eternal, unbounded by the time, space, and the matter. God is omnipotent, omnipresent and omniscient. God is the one true creator for everything with none other than himself, as his own creator. God is non-existent, yet existent, with no beginning and the end. God cannot be defined and expressed in language, but can only be experienced through the inner journey, and then understanding the engineering of the life.

CHAPTER FOURTEEN

We Are The Gods

We are the authors of our life. We write our own destinies, and nobody else. One's luck and fate are incomprehensible consequences of his or her thoughts and the actions. Do not hesitate from editing or changing the script of the life. Karma once done cannot be altered, and all its consequences shall have to be faced. It is the Law of Equilibrium. We are the images of the God. If we are the best species, then, to some extent, we are the gods. We being "the best" and superior among all species, owe the greatest responsibility to keep ourselves safe and protected, other species also safe and protected, and finally, protecting and keeping this planet and the whole creation free of harms, and beautiful. We are the tools of the God. God, the supreme energy, manifests itself through all its life forms and entities, and effects. Our relations on this planet are with all life forms, i.e. simply beyond the blood. Everything here makes our family, i.e. my biggest family. We can build and destroy anything by our thoughts and action. We are like oceans and the fire. God is the friend of silence. In silence, feel the energies and the powers inside, i.e. the God. In silence only, the God is experienced. Growth and the evolution need utter silence. God walks everywhere incognito. Godliness is a certain state, i.e. a state of mind.

States, as perceived, are creations of the mind. A being with his or her lofty thoughts, noble actions generous and magnanimous behaviour is godlike. Godliness is a accomplished state by undertaking a certain path. Those beings, which traverse this path and achieve this state, become godlike. One cannot undo the moves of the past of his life, but can definitely make the next moves of his or her life better. One's beliefs and the trust, make the possibilities limitless. A being with loving heart for all, is godlike. Life is a continuous journey. Neither, birth is the beginning, nor death is the end. Both, birth and death are transitions and transformations, i.e. transitions and transformations from non-physical to the physical, and from physical to the non-physical. Soul or the spirit, which is the true essence of every being, always exists due to his or her karma of past and present, and carry forwarded to the future. All beings are immortal. It is very difficult to make every being happy in the journey of life, but it is very easy to be happy with every being. Being god is assuming the godly traits. Best of everything is the god. Being best at few things and then trying to be best at the rest, is indication of being on the path of godliness. Life is a journey from being ordinary to becoming the extraordinary. God wants all his children to become like him. The best of everything, which lies within every being, is the God. Rise and raise this best, and become godlike. God is the quintessence of everything, i.e. the purest energy. Beings are impure energies. In the highest state of purity, energy dominates, and no matter or the material, can hold this purest form of energy (the God). God is non-physical purest effect(s). Physical life is never ending cyclic drama. It is full of pains and pleasures. But the spirit life form is full of peace and healing. Only that spirit does not embody physicality, which is pure, rest all other spirits embody physicality and reincarnate. We become God, when the whole karmic structure is being dismantled. Then, we become the existence. Karma create soul. If there is no karma, there will be no soul, and it will be complete dissolution i.e. liberation or the mukti. Body, mind and life energies get separated, and lose their existence, and merge with the grand existence during the liberation. Whole existence works in the direction of achieving the equilibrium. Never, it is in the state of equilibrium. If it is achieves the equilibrium, all process, all events will stop immediately, e.g. days and nights will never occur, change of weather will not occurs etc., and finally, the existence will cease to hold and exist. Life will also cease to exist, if equilibrium is being achieved. Equilibrium is the state of no change, no further ongoing processes. Both, life and the existence are a continuous change. In this grand existence, no two times and spaces are similar, and both of these undergo some mutation continuously, and it happens in the direction of achieving the equilibrium. Once the equilibrium is achieved, occurrence of all changes, all events, all happenings and all effects will come to end. As long as equilibrium conditions are not being met, it forces the processes to remain continuous and seemingly cyclical. There is no physical being-like God. There are processes and events in this creation, which are sustained with continuous internal and external changes, and as a part of the process of achieving the equilibrium, new processes and new events get created due to their mutual dependence and interactions, i.e. the dynamics. This whole is being conceptualised as the God. God is a figment of imagination, a creation of the mind. State of, all-perfection, being all-powerful, all-inclusiveness, and best of everything, is said to be the God. And, the essence of the life is, to become better, and better, in all life dimensions. Life is a continuous journey from current state to the state of godliness, i.e. bad to good. Improvement and growth is the purpose of the life. The component of God, i.e. improving and becoming the best, lies within all of us, and with the help of pure and conscious thoughts and the actions, the journey towards godliness is being started and undertaken. We exist here, to demonstrate our existence, to ourselves first, and to the others next. One can still be at his all-best, while believing that there is no God. God does not expect anything for itself from the beings and the other elements of his creation. One, who is all-giver, has no wishes and expectations of taking or receiving anything. It becomes our duty to be obliged and thankful to the universe, the creation, the nature, i.e. the God as believed, in lieu of everything. God is subject of belief, but one must always have a trust in his or her self-abilities. However, there is definitely an energy which prevails and pervades all over, controls, runs and manages everything (all events and processes) in this vast existence and creation. We are also the energies, and when, the two energies match, we become godlike. Becoming godlike is difficult but not impossible. Karma is the key to it.

CHAPTER FIFTEEN

Physical World And The Spirit World

I am the spirit. We are the spirits. Beings are spirits, inside the gross, or material or physical bodies. Spirit inside the body, is the real me. Beings are spirits in their physical forms. Spirit World is the true and the permanent only home of beings. Earth is the Physical World. It is a lower dimension. It is a lower vibrational level. In the Physical World, time passes quite fast. Spirit World is a higher dimension. Spirit World has a higher vibrational level as compared with the Physical World. In the Spirit World, time passes slowly. One day or one night of the Spirit World is equal to several hundreds of days or nights of the Physical World. Spirits live in the Spirit World. At the time of birth, spirit comes from the Spirit World, enters the mother's womb, and then associates itself with the embryo, and the life begins. At the time of the death, same spirit leaves the physical body of the being, and goes back to the Spirit World, which is its true home. Some spirits are unable to go back to the Spirit World, and stay on the earth, i.e. the Physical World, as ghosts due to their karma. Physical World and the Spirit World are the two worlds of transition and migration of the life. Beings have a brief stay in the

Physical World and a much longer stay in the Spirit World. Death occurs in the Physical World only, and not in the Spirit World. Beings come to the Physical World to learn and experience, and pay off their karma. It is beings visit to the Physical World, but permanent stay is there in the Spirit World only. Physical World is full of pains and pleasures, anxieties and excitements, highs and lows, and ups and downs. The Spirit World is the world of peace, joy and happiness. The world is the accumulation of the experiences, gained by the observer, as the responses to his or her thoughts, actions and the inquisitiveness. One's world is his or her life. Beings get reunited with their loved ones, who have left the Physical World, in the Spirit World. Same set of souls are repeated again and again on the earth and other physical planes in their different roles and relationships. There are many earths in this existence. The common factor connecting all things in the existence is the true love. Unconditional love is true love. In essence, we are spiritual beings. The God created the Physical World, as a place to learn. Beings are here in the Physical World, to master the process of their creation. For the normal beings, the Spiritual World is hidden. However, the Spiritual World is perfectly revealed in the Physical World. Physical World is just the beginning. The Physical World cannot exist without the Spirit World. Our minds sculpt the Physical World. What is being attracted, depends upon being's vibrations. Reunion of spirits happens in the Spirit World. Spirits, which are in the Spirit World, eagerly wait for their loved ones, who are still in their physical garbs i.e. physical bodies in the Physical World, to shed it, and come to the Spirit World, as these spirits know that Spirit World is far better place than the Physical World in every respect. The cover page of the book portrays two spirits, peeping with love, care and affection from the heavens, i.e. the Spirit World, and watching their loved one, who was in the Physical World i.e. the earth, moving out for the Spirit World after a fatal plane crash. In the Physical World, beings live in the divided families, whereas, in the Spirit World, many spirits live together, i.e. the bigger family. The Spirit World is hidden, and is not completely revealed in the Physical World. Our inner self is in the Spirit World. In order to become free, control the mind, and shut out the Physical World. In the Spirit World, beings are spirits, i.e. "the thought forms". There in the Spirit World, beings instantly manifest things just by thinking about them. Our senses are different there in the Spirit World, like seeing is through the spiritual eye. Hearing is being done telepathically in the Spirit World. Beings temporarily forget their true nature, every time when they get awake in the morning, and find themselves back in their physical bodies. Awakening in the morning is to learn the lessons here in the material world, i.e. the Physical World. Actually, we are not bodies, we are the spirits. Bodily life is the dream, a non-reality, whereas, the only reality is the spiritual thought-form. Main elements in the Spirit World are, the consciousness, the information, the energy, and the ether. Matter does not exist there in the Spirit World. Also, there is no time in the Spirit World. There is a perfect order and hierarchy in the Spirit World among the spirits, similar to that, which exists in the Physical World. The hierarchy of spirits is dependent on the level of the attained wisdom, and the achieved purity. Some spirits in the Spirit World are highly evolved teachers, i.e. angelic. Spirits differ widely in their knowledge, experiences and the morality. In the Spirit World, compassion is paramount. There is a "Hall of Records and Learning" in the Spirit World, which is quite different from anything, which can be found in the Physical World. It is possible for the beings dwelling in the Physical World to directly communicate to the spiritual entities, i.e. spirits in the Spirit World, using the expanded subtle senses, i.e. consciousness to consciousness. There are methods and techniques for it. Groups of the like-minded spirits congregate together in the Spirit World. There is perfect kinship in the Spirit World, i.e. relations "Beyond the Blood", "my biggest family". Residents in the Spirit World are as alive as beings are in the Physical World, rather more alive, effusive, exuberant and vibrant. These spirits, living in the Spirit World, had lived and died on the earth (the Physical World) many times, in the long past since the time immemorial. These spirits can very well remember all their past experiences. In the Spirit World, there is a very close connection to the very source, i.e. the God. The difference between the Physical World, i.e. the corporeal world and the Spirit World is the difference between "the receiving" and "the giving". The Spirit World is a world of bestowal, giving and the altruism, whereas, the Physical World is just opposite, with its qualities of reception, taking and the egoism. In the given life, think positive and act positive. Life is a gift. Every positive thought is a silent prayer, which transforms the life. The Spirit World is eternal, infinite plane of bliss and the knowledge. The Physical World or the material world is the plane of matter, the plane of birth, disease, old age, and the death. Spirit World is the home of the soul or the spirit. Physical World is the home of the body and the mind. Physical World is based on manifestation, thus, it is the world of objects. In the Physical World, there is a continuous change, means nothing is permanent here. There is birth, and also, the death in the physical world.

Beings continuously run behind the objects in the Physical World. In the Spirit World, there is true enlightenment, and there, beings realise that the things done in the Physical World were simply the dreams. In the Spirit World, the doer, do and the object, all three, become one, and only the real self exists there, and also, pervades there. In the Spirit World, one becomes eternal, unborn, knowledgeable and empowered. In the Spirit World, one becomes nothing and also, everything, i.e. all inclusive. The Spirit World is unimaginably better world and a place. It is a place of joy and the divinity, with a healing light, where there is a sense of truth prevailing all over. Physical World is material. Spirit World is immaterial. In the Physical World, relations and relationships are through blood, whereas, in the Spirit World, these relations and relationships are simply "Beyond the Blood". A true relation is the relation beyond the blood, which is based on true unconditional love.

CHAPTER SIXTEEN

Spirit Connections

We all are spirits, and we all are connected to one another at the spirit level, i.e. at the level of thought, or the level of consciousness. Spirit connection is the connection through the feelings. Humans are connected to humans, and also to the other things in this vast creation like the God, plants, trees, flowers, birds, mountains, rivers, sun, moon, air, fire sky, stars etc.. It is the spirit connection with them. Spirit connection is a connection, which is "beyond the blood". It creates my biggest family. Relations and the relationships at the physical level are unreal and temporary, whereas, the relations and the relationships at the spiritual level are only real, and also, permanent. Spirit is the energy. Spirit is the vibration. In this existence, everything is vibration. God is also a vibration. Communication happens when vibrations travel, and interact. Thoughts affect the quality of vibrations. Life is a thought. Everything is a thought. Thought is created inside. Thus, everything, in sense-perceptions, imagination, feelings, is a thought essentially. Thoughts travel. Thoughts are energies. Good thoughts create good energies. Bad thoughts create bad energies. We are not distinct, but one and the same. We and every other thing, has originated from the same source. We and nature are not distinct. We are the nature. Nature is us.

Live the life with inclusivity, and not the exclusivity, in order to experience the God, and the powers and the forces of the universe. In openness only, communication with the universe establishes. When the two energies match, it creates a resonance, and the exchange of energies occurs. Exchange of energies is an exchange of thoughts, feelings, good wishes etc.. Always, have hope. Hope is the life. Absence of hope is death. Hope is filled with spark and amazing potential. Spirits from the Spirit World keep sending the messages, in the forms of signs. Spirits continuously guide us during our entire journey in the Physical World. We all have very strong spirit connections. When we are ready, the Spirits from the Spirit World show us many things. Spirits send advance messages, and forewarn about the impending dangers or the difficult times. Beings are constantly guided by their Spirit Guide. A Spirit Guide is an enlightened being, now in the spirit form. A Spirit Guide is a guide to many beings at the same time. Being, which can establish conversations with the spirits of the Spirit World, is known as the Medium. Spirit messages are mostly premonitory in their nature. Heaven and the Spirit World are much more real, beautiful and lasting than this Physical World. Spirit World is filled with power and substantiality. Spirit touch is quite healing in nature. Through our spirit connections, we are inextricably connected to each other. It is one of the great powers of the universe. Spirit connections are grounded in love and compassion. Spirit connections are for real, and never die. Spirit connection is established, when one is deeply resonated with another being, or a place or a thing, and this connection always persists. The connection with the God is a spirit connection, and not the physical connection. "Integration" is complete connection with the self-spirit, and the spirit of others. Intimacy is not just physical. Feeling is communication with the spirit, the God. Feeling is the mirror of the God. Intuition is the telephone of the God. A seeker seeks the truth, by deepening his or her spirit connections. The universe shakes us, from time to time, in order to awake us, and experience and learn. Re-examine all. See all signs. Accept, what is approved by the soul, and dismiss, what insults the soul. Eliminate everything which stops from evolving. Peace and success come from within. The spirit inside, when comes in one's attention, establishes the spirit connection, leading to a power called Kundalini. As Kundalini energy rises, it balances the seven chakras, and contributes to the being's spiritual wellness. Practise of Kundalini Yoga leads to the spiritual enlightenment, which is known as Kundalini Awakening. Kundalini Yoga practise eases stress and anxiety, improves cognitive functioning, and boosts self-perception and self-appreciation. A spiritual connection is a sense that there's something bigger than the self and self-experiences, meanings, and the beliefs. Spirit connection means that we're all connected, with common goals and interests, no matter what. Soulmates are into such spirit connection with each other. Spirit is the energy, which can neither be created, nor destroyed. In the Spirit World or the heavens, such spirit connections are very easily established. Such spirits, when descend on the physical plane i.e. earth, live together, grow old together, and at the end of their journey, move on for the Spirit World together. The cover page of the books illustrates such two kindred spirits, who are now very happily living in the Spirit World, the permanent abode. Never grieve, as anything, which is lost, comes around, either in same form, or the other. Love everything. Love is the absence of judgement. Be realistic and plan for a miracle. Step out of the circle of the time, and get into the circle of the love, by establishing spirit connections, as it is the very purpose and also the essence of the life.

CHAPTER SEVENTEEN

Does Prayer Work

Prayer works, only if, the body, the mind and the spirit, are in sync. Prayer is a method of communication with the universe. For the prayer to establish, all it needs, is a certain state of the mind, the body and the spirit. Communication through prayer with the universe is established, when there is state of resonance between the vibrations of the beings and the vibrations of the universe. Prayer is an earnest request, and if it reaches the intended power, it always works. Prayer is a code, i.e. a style of utterance of certain sounds. Most of the beings do not know the technique of prayer, and therefore, their prayers remain unheard and unanswered. In the prayer, the intent of the being offering the prayer, matters most. Intentions reach every corner of the universe. Intents are one's electromagnetic radiations, which travel all over the universes. Beings with strong aura have their strong electromagnetic radiations. Life is a gift given by the God. Largely, life's aspect like birth, death and other major changes, challenges, situations and circumstances in between, all are approved by the God. Nature is the God. As a matter of fact, we create our own life profiles, life journey trajectories, from birth till death, including these, and the basis of all is karma. Karma is the exchange of energies, i.e. the debit side and the credit side of this exchange. Life drama goes on, till the whole karma is settled. We are born here to learn the lessons of the life, and pay off the karma and settle our karmic accounts. When all the lessons of the life are being learnt, and also, their learning implemented in the life, karma gets settled, and such beings then do not take birth. It is the state of Nirvana or Moksha or Salvation. Life is a big drama, full of pains and pleasures. Pains are more than the pleasures in the life. Prayer is a power in itself. When beings pray, God works for them. Prayer must be sincere. It should not be filled with needs and desires, but must be filled with the thankfulness and gratitude. Be thankful to what already we have, as truly we did not deserve even this much also. Never compare self with the others. Each being is unique, and has his or her own Pra'rabdh, i.e. the set of allotted karma for this life journey. Life is a continuous journey. Pra'rabdh is carved out of Sanchita, i.e. the accumulated karma of all life times. One's faith in the God makes his prayer to work. Power of prayer can only be experienced, and not explained. Prayers transform the life. Life has its own incomprehensible designs. Most of the times, prayers work, when nothing is going right in the life, e.g. after a great setback, there may be a sudden change of the life towards prosperity and the success. Life is a great teacher, and teaches the beings, what is just right for him or her in the life. Law of Equilibrium works in the show of the life and this vast creation. The secret of living is, "giving". If you want to shine like sun, first, burn like the sun. Kind words may be short, but are very easy to speak, and their echoes are simply endless. God always listens to us, whenever we pray. Intentions, thoughts and the spoken words travel in all the directions throughout the universe. When the frequency of invocation and the frequency of the source match, resonance occurs, and the invoked thing occurs or happens. It is the case when the prayer is being heard. God is the energy of the universes, which has certain vibrational level and the frequency. Prayer is a technique, where the state of mind and the modulation of the voice i.e. utterance profile, are quite crucial for its success. Prayer has power, i.e. the power to answer the questions. Prayer is an act of receiving the blessings of the God, which he has in store for its creation. God loves the whole creation equally. God speaks through the glory of his creations. God speaks through his Holy Spirit, through the dreams, visions and the thoughts. Prayer slows down the minds, calms the spirits, and centres the hearts. Prayer removes the minds from the surrounding culture of consumption. Prayer centres the being's energies on something greater and most important. Prayer gives a call to identify the desires, and articulate the values. God responds to the tears of everyone. In tougher times, one can easily find the strength, solace, and the comfort by crying out to the God. God eases the sorrows, and helps the beings to deal with the pains and sufferings encountered, in their journey of the life. Whenever in trouble, come to the God, with the prayer for guidance. Then, wait in the silence for the God to speak. Jot down any impression or the picture, the God gives. It is the God's answer to the prayer. Help comes rushing, whenever asked for, provided there is purity of thoughts and the heart. Life though may seem to be tougher for good beings, but in essence, good beings are truly the empowered ones, chosen by the God, for many other greater purposes. God teaches the world through his selected good beings. Prayer energizes the hearts through the power of the spirit. Consistent prayer releases the power of God's blessing in the life and its associated circumstances. If prayers are for selfish motives, driven by pride hidden in hearts, God will not answer prayers. True prayer is, when nothing is said or asked for. Prayer is said to the God, and the God is a non-physical dimension. A prayer is a method of creating a bridge between the physical and the non-physical, and it is just not that simple. A polluted mind can never offer prayers. A child's prayers will have much greater chance of being heard than an adult's prayer due to the differences of purity of their minds, leading to its acceptance or the non-acceptance by the God. Never ask for anything in the prayer. The God has already given everything, which is best deserved. Prayer is remembering the God with no favour. God already knows, what has to be done, even without one's prayer, and the best, is always served. God does not need flattery. God cannot be coaxed and cajoled. God does not need money or any kind of offering. He, i.e. the God, which has given everything to every being, does not need anything for himself. Beggars cannot be the givers. God has given us the life. God has given sweet relations, true relationships, dependable friends, brothers, sisters, mother, father, and every other needed thing. God created everything, i.e. the Spirit World and the Physical World. The God is the basis of everything, physical and the non-physical. Prayer is a longing of the soul, a longing for peace, happiness and the success. Prayer is an admission of one's weaknesses to the God. Prayers have the ability to heal. Prayers make a being less reactive to negative emotions like anger. Prayers have mental health benefits. Prayers calm the nervous system. Prayers shut down fight and flight responses in beings. Prayers eliminate depression and anxiety. True prayers always work.

CHAPTER EIGHTEEN

Beyond The Blood

True life experiences occur, and the life is lived meaningfully, only when relations are being extended "beyond the blood". Real relations are always "beyond the blood". Real relation exists at the level of souls, which is non-physical. We all are spirits, and not the body. The real we, are energies, and not the matter. Only the energy inside is permanent in us. Body keeps changing from one life to another life, but the spirit or the soul does not change, till it is dissolved finally with the supreme soul at Moksha. Moksha is release from the cycle of rebirth, which is impelled by the Law of Karma. In this creation, nobody is yours, and yet, all are yours only, rather another you. I am another you. Blood is same for all, then how it can become the bases for limited nature of the relationships, and at times leading to discrimination. If blood is the basis of all relations and relationships, then the whole humanity, and a vast proportion of the creation, is already into deeper relations and relationships, as the blood and its properties are same for all, which is running inside the all. Open up the minds. A closed mind leads to a pathetic and miserable state of the life. Happiness lies in acceptance, and not in the rejection. Happiness multiplies, when it is being divided. Real relation may not exist in a family consisting of father, mother, sister and brother, however, real relation may exist with a neighbour or a friend or a cousin or a colleague at the workplace. Some couples, or husband and the wife, may have the relationship, which is at the soul level, i.e. "beyond the blood". It is true that the marriages are made in the heaven (the Spirit World), and solemnised or celebrated on the earth (the Physical World). Real relationships are purely spiritual in nature with elements of divinity into these, "beyond the blood", i.e. non-physical. Relations are created in the Spirit World and then executed here in the Physical World. Relations are created on the basis of Law of Karma. Law of Karma is essentially the Law of Equilibrium of matter and / or energy. Real relation is caring and sharing, in its innate nature. Real relationship is based on giving, and not taking. Body is temporary, but the soul is permanent. All experiences of the life are essentially experiences of the soul inside, experienced through the body. Energy needs matter or material in order to manifest or display itself, therefore, a soul needs a physical body for experiencing, evolution and the growth. Spirits having "beyond the blood" relations, live together almost in every journey of the life. These spirits take birth in the Physical World together, die together and again take rebirth together, however, there may be some differences in their times and space coordinates of birth, death and rebirth. Relationships are worked upon in the Physical World, which creates conversion of their roles and relationships for the next life i.e. another cycle of birth and death. True love is based on the relationship, which is "beyond the blood". During accident(s), a set of spirits, leave together for the Spirit World, after their physical deaths. These beings move together to the Spirit World, in order to live together, there also together, as together they had been living on the earth i.e. the Physical World in given journey of the life. A real relationship is the blessing of the God. Every being does not get it. Life is pre scripted, and it takes its own course in order to create the relations, which are "beyond the blood", in every journey of life, on the earth or the other planet(s). There are many earths. There are many universes, i.e. multiverse. We can take birth in any universe, as chosen by us and decided and approved in the Spirit World, well before the birth in the Physical World. These universes are parallel layers or parallel levels of existence. This creation is mysterious. It is an infinite. Life, creation, and the God are beyond the limits of understanding and comprehension of normal beings. Enlightened beings can only experience it. Only enlightened beings understand the life, and live their lives in its true sense and the essence. Life partner is pre destined. One's karma determine his or her destiny. If one has created best karma in relation to his or her life partner, then he or she is destined to have the best life partner. The relation with the life partner is not through the blood, but "beyond the blood". Life is too intriguing. When in light, everything seems to be with us, but when in dark, even the shadow is not there. "Beyond the blood" brings true love and joy in one's life. And then, being feels relaxed with the other being. Being becomes a good listener. Being remains happy as the other being is around. Also, then there is an ease of communication. From both the sides, there are continuous efforts to make each other smile. There is a constant encouragement for other being's passion. "Beyond the blood" is an intense feeling of joy, and it makes one to feel very strong. Blood does not make a family, but it is the love, which makes the family. The "my biggest family" is a "beyond the blood" tie, and it is about all those beings, which share in your life, and you in theirs, with utmost love, affection and care, and with complete acceptance. "Beyond the blood" relations are well-knit together. A great relationship happens depending upon how well beings continue building the love, firstly here in the Physical World, and thereafter, in the Spirit World. True relations and the relationships, are "beyond the blood". It creates being's biggest family. True unconditional love is "beyond the blood".

CHAPTER NINETEEN

My Biggest Family

Coffee never knows that it will taste so good, before it meets the milk, and the sugar. Similarly, in the journey of life, I may be good as a being, but I become better, when I meet and blend with other right beings and other entities. Friendship and love is the biggest therapy. Magic of being together, simply cannot be defined, and cannot be contained in the logic. God is the only real head of our only real family, and this family comprises everything in this creation. God is the creator of everything. Family is a social group, a household. Family is an emotion. In the game of life, if you do not like what you are getting, change what you are giving. In the life, that which is given to the others, is only returned by them, even sometimes multiplied, may be sometimes less, or sometimes the same, and sometimes of a different form. Love invites love, hate invites hate, and anger invites dislike. Love and belongingness is family's definition. Even the most solitary soul needs someone they may call a family. A life lived in a family, filled with love and affection, compassion and care, is a well lived life. A life well lived is a life that was filled with the happiness, achievements, and the overall development. A well lived life is all about the quality and quantity of relationships. Family means anyone who gives the comforting feeling of familiarity. Family is found, and note created. Family includes parents, siblings, relatives, best friends, classmates, teachers, pets, vehicles, or even that one being, you always wave to or greet. Family is a group, of the beings, who we know accept us for us. Family stands by us all through thick and thin. One's family is his or her support system. Family keeps the one moving forward in his or her life. Family is a soul-to-soul connection. To become part of a family, is a very beautiful phenomenon. The meaning of family lies not in the blood relations, but in the relations, "beyond the blood", and is measured by the amount of love and respect held for each other. True family is based on the attributes like loyalty, selflessness, love, and genuine care and concern, e.g. a plant loved becomes the part of one's family. The expanse of one's love and care, determines the size of his or her family. A car loved, a squirrel loved, a mountain or a river that comforts one and is frequented, becomes his or her family. Family is the gift of the God to the beings. Family should not create any separation, but must demonstrate openness and acceptance. Family should not be based on exclusivity, but inclusivity. For God, the whole creation is his one family. Higher is the level of the soul, greater will be the sense of acceptance, and larger will be the size of the family. The objective of the life is to have "my biggest family". One's milieu must be his or her family. In the journey of life, one cannot move without the support of the others. Life cannot be lived without the nature and the environment. Life cannot be lived without other beings, sun, moon, wind, water, birds, animals, trees, mountains, lakes etc., therefore, all are the part of the being's family, i.e. his or her "the biggest family". One must always be concerned and careful about the wellbeing of everything in this existence. Because others are there, so we are here.

Remove all, and we will be gone. The energy of the cosmos is our life energy. Life must be lead with the utmost purity of thoughts and the actions. Life must be lead with the openness of the mind, nobility of thoughts and effectiveness of actions. Nothing belongs to anybody here. Life is an experience, experience of everything, and then gone from here. Life should not be aimed at amassing and storing the things. Nothing goes with the being, except good thoughts, good memories i.e. impressions on the mind, and the karma, which become the bases of type of rebirth. So, go out into the real world and find your chosen family. Family is a feeling one gets with others in his or her life. Family is whatever one chooses it to be, and is to be felt more than the evident. Family is a very subjective and personal experience to each and every element of creation. In the life, be thankful to everybody and everything, time and the nature, place or the situation, whether good or bad, past or present, as all these have contributed in making what you are today. Take the first step today, to let go anything bad or the negative, which is in the mind. Problems are the part of life, face these problems with smile, as it is the only art of living. Art of living is the art of dying. Trust few and with caution, as sometimes own teeth bite own tongue. Always carry childhood, in order to stay pure and young. Life begins with the family, in its true sense, where the love never ends and the hate never begins. Faith, family and friends are all alike. The creation is one big family, and we must help and care for each other. Make the family the strength and not the weakness. Family is a wonderful shelter. Bigger is the family, bigger will be the shelter. Family is all about the relationships. Sweet relations mean sweet family. Life is in relation to everything around it. Therefore, for a greater purpose of the life, give the meaning and purpose to the life, live joyfully, and find "my biggest family", wherein, all the family relations are simply " beyond the blood", and the God, is the only head of the family.

CHAPTER TWENTY

The Biggest Religion

Humanity is the biggest religion. Being human is the best act. In the Spirit Word, there is nothing like caste, creed and the religion. These are the categories that human beings have created, especially by those, which wish to remain powerful, resourceful, rich and the strong. Religions only exist in the Physical World. Human religions in the Physical World are the biggest reasons for the unrest, violence, hatred, discrimination, and a severe threat to the world's peace. There will be no other reason for annihilation of human beings other than the human beings themselves. Human beings through their nefarious acts in the name of religion will also imperil the existence of other species. God has no religion, no caste and no creed. Love is in the core of the life, and the only basis of life's existence. No caste or creed or the religion, is good or bad, superior or inferior, but it is the karma only, which is good or bad, superior or inferior. If the human beings themselves will not correct them, the nature will correct them, the God will correct them. The nature has its very harsh methods of correction. Human beings behave as if they are going to stay here for ever. In the Physical World no being is yours, yet all are yours, then why to harm others. Birth cannot become the basis of identification of the beings, but it is the thought and the action, i.e. karma, which should be the basis of everything, and in essence, it is the only basis. In the Spirit World, every being is being evaluated on the basis of his or her thoughts and actions, and the karma did, during his or her stay in the Physical World. There is one God, i.e. "only one energy", of all the universes. Then, how beings can have their own God or the gods? God has demonstrated that sun, moon, stars, planets, space, mountain, birds, trees, animals, rivers etc. are for everybody, and they treat everybody alike, then why human beings treat different beings differently. Human beings will die due to their own karma. In the show of the life, our karma affects the quality of our birth and death, and the life in-between. Life is given by the God. Life is gift. Life is the energy. Birth and the death are affected by the human karma. Birth and death are two major events of life. Neither birth is the beginning of the life, nor is death the end of the life. Life is infinite continuum and a continuous journey. All events, whether good or bad in the life, are outcomes of beings karma. In the Physical World, religion has become a socio-cultural system of certain designated texts, ethics, prophecies, behaviours, practices, morals, beliefs, sanctified places and the organisations, Religious practises in the Physical World are considered to be the methods for relating the humanity, to the supernatural, transcendental and the spiritual elements. In the Physical World, no religion is true. or good or bad. Religion is a way of understanding the God. Religion in the Physical World is a philosophy. Religion should be based on respect for the life. Beings should care about, the religion not becoming a travesty. "Goodness and righteousness" is the religion. Religion is a teaching or instilling the quality of being morally right and justifiable to / into the human beings.

Religion should be in one's heart. Be kind to all creatures. Religion is the awakening of the spirit. Religion is not the creed one professes. True religion is all about having a good heart. "Being human" is the biggest religion. Religion teaches humanity. Religion stands on morality. Religion is not worshipping, rather worshipping is only a small act out of many other religious acts and practices. Religion is not a book, but the demonstrated behaviour. Religion is not talked, but walked. The beauty one sees in the world is simply a reflection of the beauty of his or her own heart. Life is not fair and easy on any being. Life's perceived unfairness does not give the licence to one to walk the wrong and unfair paths. Life may be tough at some points. The destiny is created by the steps that are being taken. Every being has challenges in the life, to face. What is right is always known to the conscience. No matter, how much unfairness one got, or how many times one was disgraced, or how many times one had fallen, what is important, is how he or she responded to, at those moments of the journey of the life. Realisation of truth is the true religion. Morality with a dash of emotion is the religion. Religion is a revolutionary force, which opposes all negatives and the bad. Love, compassion and tolerance are the elements of the religion. Kindness is the biggest religion. God is the biggest religion. Life and the religion are not separate, but an inseparable one.

CHAPTER TWENTY-ONE

The Biggest Karma

Think good and act good. Being human is the best karma. Law of Karma is essentially the Law of Equilibrium. Any interaction between two entities creates an exchange of their energies, and good or bad karma is being created on both the sides, as the case may be. Thought is energy. Everything in the life is energy. Every act is also energy. We all here are energies. God is also energy. There are energies in the cosmos. Biggest energy exchange creates the biggest Karma, as Karma is the exchange of energies. Unconditional pure love for all is the best and biggest Karma. Love encompasses everything like peace, compassion, cooperation, empathy, kindness, caring, sharing, benevolence, magnanimity, respect, trust, faith and belief, and the experiences of the God. Best path of the life, creates the best and biggest Karma. Karma is the sum of a being's good and bad thoughts and actions, in this, and previous other states of his or her existence, which affects their future. Karma is a Sanskrit word. Karma means "action." Karma refers to a cycle of cause-and-effect. Karma refers to both, viz. the action, and also, the consequences of the action. Every action brings about a corresponding reaction. Law of Karma is a law like the Law of Gravity. Karma is the natural force of the universes. Three main types of karma are Prarabdha, Sanchita, and Kriyamana (or Agami). Prarabdha Karma is experienced through the physical body. Prarabdha Karma is a part of the Sanchita Karma. Sanchita Karma is the sum of one's all past karmas. Kriyamana Karma or Agami Karma is the result of one's current decisions and actions. Good Karma is created by loving and forgiving yourself, and also the others. Doing so prevents the beings from low self-esteem, self-blame and the self-doubt. Holding the grudges simply holds the beings back. Practise kindness and the compassion. Reflect back on the thoughts, the decisions, the actions taken, and their consequences. Karma is the result of actions and the past impressions, like a deed, a feeling, or simply an expression. Purpose directs the outcome of action(s), either positive or negative. Good deeds are rewarded either in this life or the next life. Karma determines the kind of relationships one is going to have with the others. Good Karma brings happiness. Offer compliments. Make good recommendations. Offer thanks. Teach good to the others by demonstrations. Listen to others. According to the Law of Karma, what happens to a being happens because he or she had caused it through action(s). Karma is an impersonal force. Law of Karma is "If − Then" law. Karma summarises the causal connection between actions and the experiences, and between two entities. Having the relations and relationships, and creating the biggest family, creates good Karma. Nobility of a being creates very good Karma for him or her. Everything connects with everything else. Fate is created through the actions i.e. the Karma. Nothing happens by chance in the existence, as everything is causal. Causality creates every act and every event or circumstance in the show of life. Actions create memory. This memory is only Karma. Memory travels with the mind from one birth and life to other. Actions involve exchange of energies; let it be physical action, or mental action, or the emotional action. Some or the other action is being performed by the being at every moment of the life. In order to grow, focus on the lessons. Karma is the realisation of actions. Harm comes to being, because he or she had harmed the other(s). This "other", includes every entity in the existence. If the level of consciousness is lower, lesser karmic account will be created, but with the entities having a higher level of their consciousness, a bigger karmic account is being created. Karma affects the soul, i.e. the consciousness. Good Karma travel(s) all over the cosmos, similarly bad Karma also travel(s) all over the cosmos. An average of all Karma of all beings creates a universal consciousness at a given time. What goes around comes back. Varying spaces have varying consciousness levels. The energy felt at burial grounds is different from the energy felt at the home or the house, and the energy felt at a shrine. In the Physical World, bad karma is unknowingly created along with the good Karma, however in the Spirit World, only good Karma is created. It is the reason, why there is happiness and peace all over in the Spirit World. Beings do not want to come to the Physical World, but for their karmic reasons, they are being forced to go to the Physical World. The best state in the Spirit World is the "state of bliss", which is very difficult but not impossible, to achieve here in the Physical World. A normal beings life is full of frustrations, failures, miseries, pains, upheavals, trials and tribulations in the Physical World. The life here in the Physical World is a punishment, and to learn the lessons is the only purpose of being's existence here. One's life is one's making. There is no need for any revenge or retaliation for a harm done by the other. It was our Karma, and then, by taking a revenge, why to create another bad Karma. It will then become a chain. Karma must be dissolved, and it is the devotion, which annihilates the Karma. Every entity is the reason for its creation, and also, the destruction. The secret of destruction is hidden in the secret of creation. Nothing here is for real, neither the creation, not the destruction, as both are only the ephemeral experiences, in this constantly changing infinite existence. Nothing has existed here in its previous form, but every successive form is an impression of its previous form but not the same, and it is only due to the Law of Karma. At a given time and space, only the best, and the most appropriate survives and exists. Biggest karma is not a destination, but a continuous journey, on the path of goodness, till eternity, in the show of this eternal life.

CHAPTER TWENTY-TWO

Best Emotion

"Love", is the best emotion. Love must be unconditional. In essence, love exists between the two spirits, and not between the two physical bodies. True love is spiritual in nature, and not material. True love is divine in nature. Love is the gift of the God. Love is the basis of everything, and the whole existence. Love is a power. Emotion is a strong feeling. Apart from love, anger and fear are also emotions, but these are negative emotions. In the Spirit World, there is love all over; however, in the Physical World both positive and negative emotions are present. Positive emotions create a positive personality, whereas negative emotions create a negative personality. Personality is reflected in one's attitude and the behaviour. A right attitude in the life is quite important, so as to give the life its true meaning. We do not always need a plan, but sometimes, we just need to breathe, trust, simply let go, and see what happens in the life. The most important part of one's personality is his or her speech and the spoken words. Looks can be attractive but not winning, whereas it is the speech and the spoken words, which can win the hearts of millions and billions forever. It takes just one step to change the life, but to realise the self, it may take several life times. Let us be grateful to the beings, which make us happy, as they are the charming gardeners, which make our souls to blossom. Spend more time with yourself, and you will start liking which you are. Make no bones about yourself in order to bring a positive change in the self. Positive emotions bring happiness in the life. Life is eternal, ad infinitum. Love is the most effective positive emotion. Other positive emotions are serenity, interest, hope, awe, amusement, pride and gratitude. Positive emotion is an emotional response, which expresses a positive effect, like happiness. When one attains his or her goal, or relief when a danger is averted, or the contentment when one is satisfied with the present state of affairs, he or she becomes happy. Happiness is only caused by the positive emotions. Wretchedness is caused by the negative emotions. Joy is an emotion of great happiness. Focus on the rainbows, and not on the storms, in the journey of life. One should rise in love, instead of falling in love. Until and unless, the mind is not mastered and won over, beings remain slaves of their emotions created by the mind. There are no accidental meeting between the souls; rather it is, perfectly as per the design of the life, approved by the nature, universe and the God. Souls, which live together always, are soulmates. Thoughts are the shadows of one's emotions. Keep the thoughts simple. Mind has the tendency to make the thoughts darker, and also emptier. One's expectations hurt him or her most. In true love, there are no expectations, but there is a complete commitment and surrender. It is quite difficult to find true love in these times. True love is simply "Beyond the Blood", e.g. between Krishna and Yashoda. This full existence is "my biggest family", therefore, any soul can love any other soul. We all are connected through the common universal consciousness. What one does, affects all. Expressed and unexpressed emotions both never die out. Expressed emotions do not come back, but the unexpressed emotions come back later, may be in quite distasteful and uglier ways. Be silent with those beings, which do not value your words. Do not try pleasing every being. Do not overthink. Do not fear the change. Stop living in the past. Do not put yourself down. A loving and caring soul is the gift of life. One cannot be strong all the times. Sometimes, one needs to be alone, and work on him or herself in order to improve. Display of positive emotions is the sign of strength. All emotions are the creations of the mind. Manage the mind, emotions will get managed automatically, else, emotions will manage you and your life. Never ever ignore the emotions of self and the others, and take them for granted. The beauty of the life, begins the moment, one decides to be with him or herself. Emotions keep changing for the normal beings, therefore, never take permanent decision(s) on the basis of temporary emotion(s). It is not the time, but the let go attitude of the being, which heals the wounds created due to hurtful emotions of self and the others. Never carry emotional pains unnecessarily, as there are already enough pains in the life. Our emotions are our most genuine pathways to the knowledge and self-realisation. Life is all about living in such a way, which makes its every moment, a sweet and worth carrying memory. Remember that there is "this life", and an "afterlife". Life should be enjoyable and liveable on both the sides, i.e. this side and also the other side i.e. heavens. Stay together and live together, here and there i.e. the other side, today and tomorrow, and ever and ever in this infinite life.

CHAPTER TWENTY-THREE

Best State Of The Mind

Peaceful mind is the best state of the mind with zero thought i.e. in the state of complete silence. Silence is very important in life. There is a certain sound of silence, try listening it. Sound of silence is the sound "AUM". It is the cosmic sound. "AUM" is the sound of oneness. Sound "AUM" connects the beings back to their one source. Light and sound are the bases all sense-perceptions. Light and sound are first two things, which the God had created with the creation of this existence. Life is an aggregation of sense-perceptions. If there is no sense-perception, there will be no life. Perception is the basis of all life. Perceptions are created in the mind. Mind is very powerful, and affects the life in all its dimensions and spheres. In peaceful state, one feels inner joy and the happiness. Happiness comes from pure love. Pure love is the true love which is unconditional. Unconditional love encompasses sympathy, empathy, benevolence, sharing, caring, tolerance and consideration. Happiness, which is an outcome of the peaceful mind, is a matter of one's choice i.e. his or her ways of living. Happiness is not something to be achieved, but something to be experienced. Adjust the ways of living.

Try experiencing happiness in little and big things done during the journey of life. In the Spirit World, mind always remains in its best state. In the Physical World, usually the mind does not reach its best state for a normal being. Life must be lead on the principle of "engagement with disengagement". Do not stick to anything. As everything is changing, therefore, you should also change. Cosmos is changing continuously. Change is life. No change is death. Happiness is enjoying your own company. Happiness is, living in peace and harmony with body, mind and the soul. To be happy, one does not need other beings and the material things around. Try to live alone with the self without any material thing, as it is the ultimate truth of the life. Happiness is the consequence of one's personal efforts and living a life full of purposes. Mind must be managed to remain free and unaffected of all internal and external turmoil. Master the mind. Remain in some stage of meditation all the time. Even while working, one can be in the state of mediation. Meditation is the process of maximum focus, attention and the concentration. Meditative state improves one's mental health, spiritual health and the physical health. Deeper involvement in any work, frees the being of all such factors, which can agitate his or her mind. Success and failures are mere worldly definitions, and creations of the mind. In essence, success and failure, birth and death, joy and sorrow, exhilaration and depression, elation and dejection are, only the experiences of the life, and nothing beyond that. One should remain fully calm, composed and balanced in all situations of the life. It is one's state of the mind, which creates the perception of tough or simple for the situations of the life. In the state of pure love, mind is at its best state. Mind fluctuates between thinking and engagement, depending upon the situation. Believe in the God and all acts of the God. No act of the God is bad. Biggest mistake done by the beings is that they want to lead the life as they wish, but life is given by the God, therefore, life goes the way, as the God wishes. Life has to go in sync with all the laws of this creation. There are four states of the mind, viz. random thinking or Cancalata, concentrative mind or Ekagrata, focused meditation or Dharana, and the effortless meditation or Dhyana. Good state of the mind is achieved by valuing yourself, giving up yourself, taking care of your body, setting the realistic goals, surrounding yourself with good beings, quietening the mind, breaking up monotony, and learning to deal with stress. The elements of mind are Manas or mental power or the mental faculty, Vijñāna or discernment or the consciousness faculty, and the Chitta or mind or the thought. Mind helps in knowing consciousness, and this knowing becomes being and becoming. Do not unnecessarily define the life, as these definitions may only confine the life. Freedom is the basic nature of soul and the spirit, therefore, life needs freedom. But, this freedom comes with complete accountability, and the whole set of responsibilities. Be responsible in the life for your acts and accept their outcomes, as it will bring peace to the mind in return. One's life is his or her, own creation. What happens in the life is due to his or her past or present acts. Life is infinite. Life came into the existence with this existence. Get out of low vibrational state. Do not focus on the others, but only focus on the self. Confusion is good for the life, as life is an exploration, and confusion opens up the possibilities of exploration i.e. finding. Conclusion is bad for the life. Conclusion is death. Let the mind evolve and grow. All the resources, that one needs, are within the mind. All problems are created in the mind. All solutions already exist in the mind. In fact, problems are created out of existing solutions in the mind. It is a trick of mind, played on us by the mind, in order to trouble us, and throw the being into the state of mental agitation. Mind is the friend, and also the foe, depending upon its understanding, and its management. God can only be accessed and experienced through the mind. Subconscious and unconscious minds, travel with the spirit, from one life to another. It is the reason, why we are born with certain tendencies. Mind is the memory. For the best state of the mind, memories of life must be best. The "state of life" is the "state of mind". Positive state of the mind, benefits self, and also, every other being around, and changes one's world. When the mind opens up to something new, then it never returns to the old. Be fearless. Fear is death. Mind creates fears. A right mindset must separate the best from the rest. Mindset is the general attitude of a being and their fixed ideas that are difficult to change. Peace is the fundamental requirement of the life. Happiness lies within, and not outside. Be happy with what you have, and be excited with what you wish for. Silence is never empty, but replete with all answers to all possible solutions. Silence establishes the conversation between mind and body and the spirit. Silence is needed to keep this necessary sync between the mind and body and the spirit. If speech is a river, then silence is ocean. Expansion is the life, which is outcome of the best state of mind, whereas, contraction is the death. Contraction is an outcome of the worst state of mind. Expansion of mind, consciousness and aura occurs, when one lives the life with his or her relationships, which are "beyond the blood", and with his or her thought of "my biggest family", i.e. with the nature, in full harmony.

CHAPTER TWENTY-FOUR

The Inner Transformation

Always associate yourself with the beings, which are good at their hearts, and you will experience an inner transformation. Do meditation and Yoga for the inner transformation. Meditation is inner work of self-reflection and the self-transformation. Meditation affects and works on the three basic elements, viz. mental, physical and the emotional elements. Meditation is a practice, which uses techniques like mindfulness, focusing the mind on a particular object or a thought or an activity. Meditation increases the levels of attention and the awareness. Through meditation, one can very easily achieve a mentally clear and an emotionally calm and a stable state. Yoga is the science of inner transformation. Yoga is a system of exercises for the body mainly involving breath control. Yoga relaxes both, the mind and the body. Inner transformation is a silent revolution. Have self-realisation. Inner transformation relates to various aspects of existence, and interactions. Inner transformation includes beliefs, values, mindset, consciousness, worldviews, spirituality and connectedness with the nature and the existence. Inner transformation eliminates anxiety, negativity, panic attacks and depression. With little practise, mind management, positive thinking and attitude correction, one can very easily reshape his or her thinking patterns, such that negative thoughts do not arise again. We create and choose our own thoughts and no one else. As we grow, we change, and as we change, we grow. Inner transformation is an internal shift, which brings one in alignment with his or her true highest potential. Inner transformation is a processes comprising, realisation, release, rebound, reinventing, resurrection and response. Declutter and detox the self, for the purpose of inner transformation. Re-examine the beliefs. Be conscious. Expand the mind. Go outside and interact with the nature. Take care of self. Learn to let go. The process of inner transformation is a process for well-being based on the science of Yoga. Inner transformation brings about personal growth by shifting the way one perceives and experiences his or her life, work, and the world around. Inner transformation demands of beings, metanoia, repentance, and a complete change of their hearts. Metanoia is the process of changing the mind, which eventually, changes one's life. Tantra practise brings about inner transformation. Tantra is a spiritual practice. Tantric practices touch upon all aspects of earthly life leading to the spiritual realization. The essence of the Tantric practice is going into everything, as completely as possible, in totality with complete consciousness. Inner transformation is a journey of self-discovery, e.g. who we are, why we are here, what was before, what will come after etc.. Inner transformation is the process of self-elevation through patience and struggle. Inner transformation starts with the changed understanding about the environment and the milieu, and then, changes the outer or external relationships. After that, we go deep, and starting working on the inner elements. All problems of the life can be easily solved through the process of inner transformation. Inner transformation raises the being to new and a higher level of the consciousness through the process of moving from unwillingness to the willingness. Inner transformation leads to awakening. Being's choices and the decisions create his or her life. One's honest efforts for inner transformation are greatly supported by the Akashic Intelligence. Akash means space. Space is a mysterious element. It is one of the five fundamental elements, which hold the life. Akashik intelligence holds the whole cosmos together. Akashik intelligence is the womb of all creation. Akashik intelligence is the womb of all intelligence. Akashik intelligence is the intelligence of creation, about, what is happening around. Akashik intelligence is accessible to all, and not denied to anyone, and all it needs is a certain state of mindfulness, i.e. alertness, i.e. certain level of increased consciousness, in order to receive it. If the God answers the prayers, then he increases one's faith in him, i.e. the God, but if the God delays the answers of prayers, then he is increasing one's patience, and if the God does not answer the prayers, then he has definitely something better to give. God knows every being's capability. God knows the complete life plan of every being. For those beings, which put their best and sincerest efforts, God wants that such beings should not settle for less. God knowingly makes the life of good, honest, sincere, dedicated, ethical and moralistic beings more and more challenging and tough, as he, i.e. the God, very well knows that he or she (being) can do much better than this. Problems in the life are only for the purpose of self-improvement, and nothing else. No problem is really a problem, as it is only the creation of one's mind, and then, any problem is not going to continue or persist, as it will change soon. In this creation, everything is changing at every moment. Time holds the treasure. Being's intelligence should work for him, and not against him. Life gives ample opportunities to know, and to learn, as knowing and learning creates experiences; and the life is all about experiencing the things which come its way. Be stable and still like a mountain. Inner transformation is a journey up to divinity. Get pure and more pure; become the nature and the cosmos will be yours. Live with the relationships, which are "beyond the blood", and create "my biggest family". Love every other thing, fully and unconditionally. All is for you, and yours. He is another me. This whole creation is you and yours, then why to live in exclusivity. Have a magnanimous character. Adopt all, embrace everything, and then witness the magical transformations happening in the life, the inner lotus of the life blossoms then. Peace prevails with happiness all around, and you become god.

CHAPTER TWENTY-FIVE

The State Of Death

Mind also exits along with the spirit during the death of the body. Spirit carries the mind with itself. The mental and emotional states at the time of death, as contented or joyful or miserable, create impressions on the mind, which later decides being's next course of life (rebirth), i.e. type of birth, time of birth, space of birth, type of family, type of health, duration of the journey of life, and everything associated to it. Mind carries all impressions and memories of all previous lives. Stay patient, and trust your journey of life. Mind is not a dustbin. Do not keep jealousy, hatred or anger into it. Mind is a treasure box. Keep sweet memories, happiness and unconditional love into it. Death is classified as natural or accidental or a suicide or homicide or undetermined, or pending. During the death, heartbeat and blood circulation slow down. The brain and organs receive lesser oxygen than they actually need. Consciousness contracts and life forces with start withdrawing. All this happens with the approval of the nature. Brain and other organs work less in the state of death, and eventually stop to cause the death. During the days before the death, beings start losing control of their breath. Beings become calm and still in the hours, before they die. In the state of death, beings close their eyes, or they might be half-open. Facial muscles relax. Jaw drops. Skin gets pale. Breathing alternates between loud rasping breaths and quiet breathing. Towards the end, dying beings breathe periodically, with an intake of breath, which may be followed by no breath for some time. Being seems to stop breathing only to start it all again. There might be one or two last gasps per minute, and then there is the last breath. Samadhi is an act of consciously and intentionally leaving the physical body. Samadhi is death. Samadhi is the highest state of consciousness. Samadhi is achieved through deep meditation. In Samadhi, one attains spiritual enlightenment. In enlightenment, the real self, mind, and the object of meditation, all merge together into one. "Dying while living" is experiencing the death while living. "Dying while living" is the withdrawal of the consciousness, from the mundane to the higher aspects of the being. The moment of someone's death is often very profound. In the state of death, one prefers to be alone. In the state of death, some beings feel overwhelmed with sadness, for others it may take time to process how they feel. Every being's experiences of dying are quite unique. The concept, "Dying while living", has its seeds in the Vedic literature. "Dying while living" entails cleansing the heart and the mind. This cleansing of heart and the mind is done by chanting prayers, divine names and effacing the ego. Meditation and practices of mindfulness help one to live in tune with the universal soul, and then unfold the natural energy of the self. During the process of achieving unitary consciousness, being's body is detached from his or her mind, and he or she loses awareness about itself without being cut off from the vital energy, which is propelling it. "Dying while living" is the voluntary death from which one can resurrect, after experiencing a new life, only to create blissfulness further in the reaming journey of life. During this deeper state of meditation, i.e. "Drying while living", one transcends the time and the space. He or she partakes of the music of the soul. He or she bathes him or herself in the luminosity of the higher self, i.e. the self of all, the divine, the God. There are infinite possibilities to transcend the physical plane and explore the realms of spirits. There are out of body experiences (OBE) and near death experiences (NDE) preceding the death. Death is a transition, i.e. a transformation. In the state of death, some beings see their guardian angel, other angels or the spirits, and also, their relatives, which had departed before him or her, welcoming the dying being, and ready to take him or her to the other side. Death is peaceful for some, but painful for many others. There is grief, regret and repentance in the state of death, but now, nothing can be done. One should have a peaceful state of the mind at the time of death. In Tibet, Bardo is the process carried out in the state of death. Bardo is the state of existence, intermediate between two lives on the earth. Bardo is a state of existence between death and rebirth. Bardo varies in length according to being's conduct in his life and manner of, and the age at death. In Bardo, the dying being is told to remain calm and peaceful, and a halcyon atmosphere is being created for him or her to depart. In Bardo, the dying being is told, not to make hurry for next birth, i.e. rebirth, and choose his parents, family, place, time etc., quite carefully and comfortably. There are four types of liberation, viz. Salokya, Samipya, Sarupya and Sayujya. In Salokya, one stays in the eternal felicity of god's world. In Samipya, one is in close contact with the god. In Sarupya, one attains likeness with the God. In Sayujya, one savours the bliss of identity with the God. In Sayujya, one feels

"Ekatva", i.e. the oneness with the God. Such enlightened beings (Sayujya), emit a beatific aura, which has its impact all around. To achieve such an enlightened state, it is not necessary to renounce the family and the possessions, or to start living on the mountains, or in a cloistered surrounding. It is also not necessary to wear specific dresses or to put on any religious insignia. Nitya Mukta beings are eternally liberated, and perform divinely ordained tasks. Nitya Mukta beings are inwardly free from all desires. Nitya Mukta beings are outwardly very active in their lives. Nitya Mukta beings are quite detached. Nitya Mukta beings are full of creativity and zeal. Nitya Mukta beings live the life as Sakshi, i.e. the witness. They are witness to what is going on in the world. Such Sakshi beings, maintain equipoise in all situations, whether favourable or hurtful. Nitya Mukta beings, even after attaining Siddhi, i.e. the supernatural power, by abiding in the self, do not boast of anything, as it might dilute their inner progress and the power. Death is an illusion. Death is an honour. Death is a gift. Death is an opportunity. Death is the liberation. Death is the freedom. Death must be graceful. The real "Art of Living" is the "Art of Dying".

During The Death

During the death, life forces withdraw themselves from all corners of the physical body, the consciousness inside contracts from all the parts of the physical body, limbs get numb and paralysed, and finally, the consciousness exits the body. Natural death is not a sudden process, but a gradual process. Death knocks at the door several months before. Reverse the process of the birth; it will become the process of the death. Birth is the entry of soul into the body; death is the exit of soul out of the body. In normal course, similar to the birth, death is also a process involving nearly nine months. Death is a beautiful experience of the life, a major transformation of the life, i.e. change of physicality into non-physicality. Even the subtle body or the astral body is little physical. Causal body and bliss body are non-physical. When a being comes to the life, it is already old enough to die. Death is like changing the clothes. Death is already decided with the birth. The type of death is according to the karma of being. Only death is certain in the journey of life, and rest everything is uncertain. After the death, spirit of the being goes to its realm. One is born here in the Physical World to pay off and or settle his or her karma. If there is no karma left, there will be no birth either, and therefore, no death also.

It is called salvation or Moksha, i.e. the ultimate liberation. Moksha is release from the cycle of rebirth. Moksha is impelled by the Law of Karma. Moksha is the transcendent state, which is attained as a result of being released from the cycle of rebirth. Life and death are same, and can only be understood after understanding the other. Spirit always wants to liberate itself that is why; it is born and reborn after every death. Soul or the spirit wants freedom. The times of birth and the death can only be decided by the self-realised and enlightened beings, as they develop this ability through certain practices. Life is eternal. There is nothing like death in the life. The curiosity to know the death, expands one's awareness, and gives a bigger and higher dimension to the life. Spirit is soul with certain physicality. Soul is purely non-physical. Consciousness with certain attributes like, desires, likes and dislikes, tendencies, happiness and unhappiness, meeting, uniting and merging, jealousy, aversions etc., becomes soul. These attributes and tendencies create the type and kind of the soul like, good soul or the bad soul, pure or unsullied soul and impure or sullied soul. Soul is the life force. Soul expresses or manifests itself through the body, which it has acquired. Energy needs matter to manifest itself. Manifestation is the ability to create physical effects. Death for normal beings is quite painful and distressing process. It is equally painful and traumatic for the beings attending the dying being. Death may occur due to accident, or sudden cardiac arrest, or due to serious disease in the intensive care unit of a hospital. Pains of dying being help him or her, in detachment from the loved ones, wealth and possessions, and the other things of this material world, and the being remembers the God and wishes to embrace the death, as he or she knows that now it is the only way of comfort now by elimination of excruciating physical, emotional and mental pains. During the death, being goes into full flashback of his or her this lived journey of life, moments and the memories, the halcyon days of past, and then, suddenly tears start rolling down from the eyes. During the death, being knows that now it is the time to say goodbye, and to move on. The dying being comes to know the design of the life. This move on, helps his soul or spirit to evolve. Death is fixed, and the time and type of death cannot be changed, in the case of normal beings. Death for all must happen in peace. Attending beings should not wail over the present state of the dying being. In the life, beings can only make efforts. A sincere effort is the biggest karma. Results of efforts are not within control of beings. Decision(s) will never be perfect; however a sincere effort should always be done to take a possibly right decision. When one dies, he or she has Near Death Experience (NDE), and the Out of Body Experiences (OBE). Dying being is attended by the spirits, and consoled, and encouraged to proceed. Spirit sees its body lying dead on the bed or in the pool of blood, and the wailing relatives standing or sitting around. The spirit tries to communicate with the loved ones, but it is unable to communicate with them, as they are quite overwhelmed. For the spirit, it is very frustrating situation, as already it has lost its physical body, and unwilling to understand that it has died now, and over that, there are sad and wailing relatives and the family members. For spirit also, it is an emotionally challenging situation. Spirit tries reaching out to family members, friends and the relatives, and wishes to establish communication with them at all costs, but is unable to do it, as now, the spirit had no physical body, and the communication is not that simple, as it used to be, when it was in its physical body. However, spirit is able to communicate at the level of the minds, i.e. the level of thoughts. Thoughts create ideas. An idea is a picture or an impression in the mind. On the emotional front, death is the worst situation of life. To handle it, beings should be emotionally stable, and must understand "what is the life". The most difficult task is to make every being happy, but it is quite simpler task to be happy with every being during the journey of life. The tongue has no bones, but it is quite strong to break the hearts, therefore, be careful with the spoken words. Things which cost peace are too expensive, therefore, we must learn to let go. Learn to behave well with others. Anxiety happens, when one thinks that, he or she has to figure out everything all at once. Breathe and relax. Believe in your strengths. Worry and concern are different. Worried being sees the problem, whereas, the concerned being solves the problems. Become more and more stable in the life. Consciously behave with all during the journey of life, such that, there are no regrets, repentances and the sorrows. Death is actually not a loss. Beings always live in one's memory, subconscious and the unconscious mind. One can always reach to a dead loved one, through his or her subconscious mind. Inner talk establishes the communication with the dead being. Memories never die. Love never dies. Pain felt, is due to the love, but in the state of true love, i.e. the unconditional love, there should be no pain. Be thankful to the God, the nature, the existence for bringing that being in the life. Every being comes with his or her fixed journey of the life. Birth brings the death, and then, death brings the next birth, i.e. the rebirth, and thus, the drama of the life and the existence, goes on. Everything, every process is cyclical in the nature, and not linear. Things appear and reappear in their transformed states and forms, infinite number of times. Beings are needed for the existence. As we are due to this existence, this existence is also due to us. Beings, which truly love each other, handle the death quite gracefully. Death is a fiction, a fallacy. Death is simply the movement into another dimension of the life. A life well lived brings a happy death.

CHAPTER TWENTY-SEVEN

After The Death

Beings pass through a light tunnel after the death. On the other side of the tunnel, there is Spirit World. A complete life review of the dead being in the presence of his or her spirit takes place there. It is attended by the angels, and other elder spirits. Mistakes of being are told in this life review process. New objectives for the new journey of life are being set. It all happens in the Spirit World in the presence of senior spirits, angels and the guardian spirits. After the death, the loved ones, which are left behind on earth, should never wail or lament over or mourn the death of the departed being. Death is a promotion of the being, which has died. Never feel guilty or blame self for incorrect decisions or inactions or unfilled desires and wishes of the dead being. We all come with certain fate and destiny, which is inexorable and invincible. Remember, those who are present today, will also die one day, and then, we meet again in the Spirit World, and then after some time, back in the Physical World. Death is an endearing experience, full of comfort. Death is a profound experience about the true self. Secrets of the life are hidden. Death is the lap of the nature, i.e. the lap of the God. Nature is the mother of all mothers. Death coordinates about time, type and place are irrevocable, i.e. fait accompli. Beings, which are left behind, should wish a good life journey ahead for the departed soul. Soon, we shall meet them. Death is a fallacy. There is nothing like death, but life and only life. What is physical may vanish, but that, which is non-physical will never vanish, as these are energies. Energy can neither be created nor destroyed. Out of five bodies of beings, a layer behind another layer, the three bodies or koshas, viz. Annamaya (physical body), Pranamaya (energy body) and the Manomaya (mental body), are physical, whereas, the remaining two bodies or koshas, viz. Vijnanamaya (supramental body) and the Anandamaya (bliss body), are non-physical. The Annamaya Kosha or the physical body is earthly accumulation created by eating food. It is the physical sheath or the outer layer. The Pranamaya Kosha is life force sheath and quite vital, and it includes breath. The Manomaya Kosha is contained within the Annamaya Kosha and the Pranamaya Kosha. Vijnanamaya Kosha connects the physical bodies with the non-physical bodies. Anandamaya Kosha is the last layer. Anandamaya Kosha is closest layer to the Atman or the soul. Anandamaya Kosha is closest to the God. These are the five bodies of the consciousness. The Causal body or Karana Sarira is the highest innermost body, which veils the Atman or soul or the true self. Death is a natural process of life. Death can happen in two ways, viz. untimely death, say by committing suicide or by accident or due to sudden sickness, and the timely death. Timely death means the death when the time of this journey of life is complete. Spirits of those beings, who have met untimely death, stay in this physical world, and complete their allotted time period, in the non-physical state. Ghost is a non-physical state. After the death, every being becomes ghost. Some beings, who have met their timely death, stay in the ghost state for a less time, as compared to those, who have met untimely death. After the death, when soul leaves the physical body, the body becomes too light, as if it is floating in the air, with all anxieties and pains gone. Senior spirits or elder spirits, or the spirit guide, then hold the spirit of the deceased being, and take it to the Spirit World. We all live our lives at different levels. The state of death depends on the karmic account of being. Every being has a unique state of body, mind and emotions at the time of his or her death. Beings do not want to die. Beings have a deep-rooted attachment with physical body. Soul or spirit keeps hovering on the body, and does not want to leave the body. Spirit sees lamenting family members, relatives and friends. Spirit wishes to communicate with them, but cannot do it using the physical means like before, when it had not died. The only way to communicate after the death is through the mind, but the beings attending the body are so overwhelmed with grief, that they are unable to receive such a communication from the spirit of the deceased being, which is trying its level best to reach up to them. The spirit of the deceased being tries to communicate with, and console, the wailing family members, relatives and friends. This world is not truth, and so are its associated experiences. Nothing is a reality here. We are live in an unreal world of existence. No event is for real here. For meditative beings, death is a very pleasurable experience. Spirituality is the way and art of living, as it helps in living a meaningful life. A silver cord connects the spirit with the physical body through navel, and when, it is severed, death occurs. During astral travel, the spirit remains connected with the physical body through this silver cord. Dreams are naturally occurring astral travelling experiences. Such experiences also occur in the deeper states of meditation and Out of Body Experiences (OBE). Past Life Regression (PLR) is a very simple hypnotic way of experiencing the death in the past lives. Near Death Experience (NDE), solves the mysteries behind the process of death, states and processes before the death, and the states and processes after the death. Angels attend the death of good beings, and accompany their spirits during the onward journey. Spirits try to enter its body, which has been shed just now. Spirits which refuse to go the Spirit World remain on the earth, i.e. the Physical World, in their subtle bodies, as ghosts. Such spirits remain near to their house, near to their family members. Many times, such spirits help their family members and others, which are in their physical bodies, and not yet died. But many times, such spirits bother and trouble the beings, who have not yet died. To fulfil their earthly desires, such spirits, which are now ghosts, possess a being having a weaker aura, and through him or her, satisfy their physical senses and pleasures. The possessed being, gradually loses his or her health, and then die after some time, if not exorcised. After the death, spirit passes through a tunnel. A divine healing light is seen on the other side of the tunnel. It is the passage to the Spirit World. After the spirit reaches the Spirit Word, after the death on earth, it is given rest for some time. The spirit is healed during this time. Then after the healing, a life review takes place, where senior and elder spirits tell this spirit about the follies committed. A spirit has no gender. The spirit is taught new lessons and given fresh instructions. Then, the spirit is made ready for the next physical life, i.e. rebirth, in the Physical World. There are many earths in this cosmos. On permission, the spirit is allowed to visit its home, see and interact with its family members, relatives and the friends who are left behind in the Physical World. On occasions, like festivals, feasts, worships, birthday celebrations, marriages, arrival of new member in the family during the birth etc., such spirits reunite with their families, relatives and friends, and attend the moment. It is the reason, why special vibes are being created and felt by others, on such occasions. Only love is permanent and real. Love is the basis of everything, and also, of this creation. Hatred should have no place in the life. After some time, this spirit reincarnates itself, as per the divine calculations, at certain time and space, amidst certain beings, depending upon its karma exchange. We all affect each other always. Life is exchange of energies, i.e. exchange of karma. When some being is born, or someone dies, there is full consent of all getting affected, of which usually we do not remain consciously aware of. Whether in the Physical World or in the Spirit World, a being remains surrounded by several beings. As we have a family here in the Physical World, similarly, we all have a much bigger and more loving family there in the Spirit World. Death must be respected. Death is reassuring and not intimidating. Death is the design of the nature for betterment of beings, to leave the old, and adorn the new. Death breaks the monotony of the life. Death is the reason for many to believe in the existence of the God. Remove the fear of death. Death is a divine arrangement. Death is necessary for birth. All processes including the birth and the death are cyclical, in nature. In this existence, at every moment, many things and beings die, and many things and beings are born, and reborn. This is how; the God has designed this existence. Value those, who add value to your life. Stay where your presence is valued, and your absence is missed. The size of the success in the life depends on the depth of desires. In the game of life, reset, readjust, restart and refocus as many times as needed, but never quit. Lovely times of the journey of the life do not come back, but lovely relations and the golden moments with lovely beings stay in the hearts of beings and this creation, for ever and ever. We all are immortals. What dies, is not the true self, and the true self can never die. The true self of every being is the element of the God. Nothing and no being can die here in this creation. The death of things and beings is the death of creation. Death is a change, a change of the form. Birth is also a change of the form. Death is a fiction, the biggest illusion of life. Live the life, by creating the relations and the relationships, "beyond the blood", in "my biggest family", as it defies the death, and embraces the life.

CHAPTER TWENTY-EIGHT

We Will Meet Again

We will meet again in the Spirit World after the death, and then again back in the Physical World, after taking a new birth, i.e. rebirth. We all exist apart from our mortal physical bodies. Physical body is only a garment. We all are immortal souls, children of the God. Consciousness is eternal. Death is temporary emancipation. Beings look upon the death with utter dread and painful sadness. But all those beings, which have died, now know that death is a wondrous experience of peace and freedom. Death is freedom from limitations of the physical body. It is the death, which makes one to realize, how free he or she is. Immediately after the death, there is a sense of fear of the unknown, and the death seems to be bit unfamiliar to the consciousness. But soon, little after the death, there is a great realization, and the soul feels a joyous relief and the ultimate freedom. Death is a state of rest. Laugh at the death, when it comes. Death is also an experience like many other experiences of the eternal life. Life is infinite, a continuous journey. Actually, no being can ever die. Soul is the real self, and it is immortal. Our existence is eternal. We are needed for this existence. We make this creation of the God. Creation exists even after one is gone, which itself proves that we are not really gone, as the creation still exists, because we make this creation. We are like the waves, which come to the shore, and then go back to the sea, but it is not lost. This wave becomes one with the ocean, and then after some time, again returns to the shore as another wave. It is birth, death and rebirth of the wave, so is our story. In each journey of the life, there is a new allotment of a life role and a new script of the life. Life is an experience. Only, the physical body vanishes at the death, but the soul essence within, never ceases to exist. Even matter is also indestructible like the energy. Actually, the physical body is also not gone anywhere after the death and all the rituals are over, only it is scattered in the nature now, and not in the form, as we knew it before. Soul or spirit or the consciousness is energy. Matter undergoes a continuous change. Life is a continuum, a continuous series of journeys of life, in which each one journey is only slightly different from the next journey next, but two far off journeys in this continuum are too different from each other. Physical body is matter. Birth and death both, are the experiences of change of matter, whereas energy remains the same, unaffected, called as Atman or the soul or the spirit or the consciousness. Physical death cannot destroy our spiritual essence. There is nothing like death in reality. It is a society made convention. When one gets tired of the life, he or she simply takes off this overcoat of this flesh, i.e. the physical body, and goes back to the astral world. Spirit World is the astral world, where all spirits live in love harmoniously. Law of Karma is the law of justice. Birth and death occur as per one's karma. Death is a welcome rest. Mortality is a dream, a delusion. God is never cruel, but always too merciful. The consciousness of dying being finds itself light and relieved of the weight of the physical body. The consciousness finds that now there is no necessity to breathe, and also, there is no physical pain. There is a sense of soaring through a tunnel, which is very peaceful and there is hazy and dim light inside the tunnel, but a bright attracting light on the other end. The consciousness then drifts into a state of oblivious sleep, which is deeper and enjoyable. In the Spirit World, souls are clothed in gossamer light. In the Spirit World, all forms of vibrations function in harmony with one another. In the Spirit World, souls live in peace, mutual cognizance, cooperation and the conscious helpfulness. Everything in the Spirit World is made up of the living light. There in the Spirit World, souls drink and eat orange rays. There in the Spirit World, souls live in complete joy and peace. "Life After Death (LAD)", i.e. afterlife is too glorious. Our thoughts give our departed loved ones, a sense of well-being, and a sense of being loved. Therefore, send thoughts of love and goodwill to the departed loved ones. Mentally tell them, "We will meet again". Reassure them of continuing the divine love for them. If we keep sending our loving thoughts to them continuously, someday we will surely meet them again. This journey of the life is not the end of the life. The life is a link in the eternal chain of our relationships with our love ones. Soul meets its friends and the relatives from the life they just lived after exiting its body. Souls, called "greeters", come and attend the dying being, and help him or her, in this transition, known as the death. Souls always exist in 'soul groups" or 'soul families", both in the Physical World and also, in the Spirit World. These souls often incarnate together. Souls share numerous lives, in the past, at the present, and also, in the future. There had been many reporting of seen and experienced spirits leaving together for the Spirit World after an accident. Spirit rises from its physical body. Spirit sees its dead physical body lying on the bed in the hospital ICU, or lying in a pool of blood on road in an accident, or totally charred to death in a plane crash. It is the cover page photograph of this book. Also, two loving souls are also shown up in the heavens. There is a definite afterlife after the death on the other side. This creation has innumerable dimensions of its existence, with life everywhere, in all dimensions. We all are spiritual beings. We are here on the earth, temporarily for learning few allotted life lessons, which needs material form. Even, while living on the earth, one can meet his or her loved ones living in the Spirit World, in dreams. Dreams are gateways to spiritual realms, while we're still in the physical form on the earth, i.e. the Physical World. We are being greeted by our deceased loved ones upon the death. Dying beings are often visited by their mothers. Mother is the being, which is present at all thresholds of the life, i.e. first breath (birth) and the last breath (death). The dying being encounters visions. Vision is an experience of seeing someone or something in a dream state, or state of trance, or as a supernatural apparition. Hands seem to be passionately reaching upward to some unseen force. After death, up in the heavens, there is an incredible reunion with all those, we had loved, and were lost. God exists. Evil is the absence of life, faith and true belief in the God. It is God's designed creation, too intrigue, but too mysterious, and simply beyond comprehension. Many things of the life are beyond the logic and the comprehension. Birth is a miracle, which brings us into a journey of life in the Physical World. Deathbed visions are also a miracle. Dreams while being alive, and the visions just before the death, carry us through the death, into the next part of our eternity.

CHAPTER TWENTY-NINE

Up In The Heavens

The Astral World or the Heavens, i.e. the Spirit World, is the dimension, where the soul goes at its death. Up in the heavens, spirits enjoy such a freedom, which they had never known before during their earthly life. The passage, up to the heavens, is through a dark spiral tunnel. Heavens is misted up in white clouds. Loving and caring spirits live together in the heavens. There is a healing divine white light on the other side of the tunnel. There is "Garden of Bliss", up in the heavens. All around, up in the heavens, there are shining milky water falls. Heavens is filled up with healing lights and mesmerising aroma. There are nectar filled fruits, up in the heavens. Life after death is too beautiful, glorious and comforting. No more one has to lug about this baggage of bones, with all its troubles, up in the heavens, as it is the place for the spirit, and not for the physical body. Heavens is a place of eternity. Earth, i.e. Physical World is a place of mortality. Being is completely free in the astral heaven, unhindered by any physical limitation. Whenever a dear one dies, do not grieve unreasonably. Try to understand that he or she has gone on to a higher plane at the will of God. God knows what is best for every being. Rejoice that the soul is free now, up there in the heavens. Pray so that that your love and goodwill encourage the soul to move forward on the path of progress. Cherish good memories of togetherness. Thank them for being a part of your life, and making the life a fulfilling exciting experience. Thank the God. Do not keep the spirits or the souls earthbound by unjustifiable selfish attachments. Extreme sorrow and grief prevents the departed soul from going ahead towards greater peace and freedom. The moment, thought of our loved ones, which are not in their physical form now, enters our minds, they get available to us, listen to us, love us, care for us, and also, respond to us as best they can, within the confines of this existence. Many times, we are unable to receive and interpret their messages, as we are filled with great sense of loss, remorse, regret and the grief, or may be due to stubbornness and disbelief. Love transcends everything, and is simply beyond the life and death. Our loved ones are always with us no matter what. They always try reaching out to us, guide us and console us. Love is eternal. Love is the only bond, which ties two entities in this creation. Do good to others, as it always comes back in unexpected ways. Every sorrow is healed, up in the heavens. While on the earth, heavens is a choice, a way of living the life, and not any particular place. Heavens while on earth, is within us, and not outside. Heavens is a dimension, where angels live. Prayer is the key to the heavens, and the faith unlocks the door of heavens. God created the heavens and the earth. Loved ones visit us during in our dreams. They can assume any form, as they desire. After death, there is a life review process, during which, one realises that how loving or hurtful he or she had been to others, while living on the earth. Spirit guides surround and comfort the spirit during this life review process. One is asked to judge him or her for the acts done. Upon death, the soul rises out of the physical body. Soul dissociates its strong connection, which it had with the body, which it had mistakenly identified as the self, during the journey of life on earth. We all return to the Spirit World upon death, i.e. our real home, and keep taking different life forms and times, as we are born again and again, i.e. reincarnation, in order to continue our spiritual evolution. Heavens is a dimension, where beings such as gods, angels, saints and venerated souls reside. Heavens is a dimension of peace, love, community and the worship. Heavens is a parallel realm, where everything operates according to the God's will, and the being does not have his or her freewill, as exercised by him or her, while on the earth. In this existence, there are seven upper worlds, viz. Bhuloka i.e. Earth, Bhuvarloka, Svarloka, Maharloka, Janarloka, Tapoloka and Satyaloka, and also, seven lower worlds, viz. Atala, Vitala, Sutala, Talatala, Mahatala, Rasatala and Patala. We go to any one of these fourteen dimensions, depending on our karma. Life is simply incomprehensible, as, from where we had come, where we will go, why we are here on the earth, etc. are few of the many questions, which are not answered directly by the universe, but in the state of enlightenment. As a normal being, one does not have many choices, except, keep performing things with positive thoughts. Behave well with others. We all are trapped here in this creation. It is the design of the life and the creation by the God. Love everything and every being unconditionally. We remain and live together up in the heavens. Heavens is a state of mind, and if, earth life had been good, then only afterlife will also be good. Goodness of the life is very less physical, but more religious and spiritual in its nature. Loved ones remain together here on the earth, and also, up in the heavens. We eagerly keep waiting other loved ones, which are still on the earth and continuing their journey of life, for their arrival up in the heavens, for a grand reunion. Here on earth, life is full of sorrows, and the biggest sorrow is death. Though life is full of pains, yet, no one wants to die. Birth and death are the creations of the God. God is never discriminatory, but all loving and caring. God is our spiritual parent. Dedicate everything to the God. Pain is felt due to our attachment and association. Understand the design of the life. Life is a continuous journey. Death is the biggest cosmic joke and an illusion. Live the life, not as a player, but as a spectator and a witness. God will make us to play, as and where needed and required, without conscious thoughts and efforts. Life is, what happens to it, when, we are planning something else. Bad happens suddenly unexpectedly in the best times of the life, it is the life. Big events of the life cannot be managed and controlled. Train and manage the mind, so as not to give distress by creating anxieties and worries, but to give solace and the inner peace. Do Yoga and meditation, as it is the way of life, while living on the earth. Every struggle in the life, shapes us into a better being, therefore, be thankful to the tougher times of the journey of life, which made us strong, wiser and awakened. Live, with the relationships "beyond THE BLOOD", in "my biggest family", as it is the God's will, and also, an order, for each one of us.